SpringerBriefs in Computer Science

SpringerBriefs present concise summaries of cutting-edge research and practical applications across a wide spectrum of fields. Featuring compact volumes of 50 to 125 pages, the series covers a range of content from professional to academic.

Typical topics might include:

- A timely report of state-of-the art analytical techniques
- A bridge between new research results, as published in journal articles, and a contextual literature review
- A snapshot of a hot or emerging topic
- An in-depth case study or clinical example
- A presentation of core concepts that students must understand in order to make independent contributions

Briefs allow authors to present their ideas and readers to absorb them with minimal time investment. Briefs will be published as part of Springer's eBook collection, with millions of users worldwide. In addition, Briefs will be available for individual print and electronic purchase. Briefs are characterized by fast, global electronic dissemination, standard publishing contracts, easy-to-use manuscript preparation and formatting guidelines, and expedited production schedules. We aim for publication 8–12 weeks after acceptance. Both solicited and unsolicited manuscripts are considered for publication in this series.

**Indexing: This series is indexed in Scopus, Ei-Compendex, and zbMATH **

More information about this series at http://www.springer.com/series/10028

Shriphani Palakodety · Ashiqur R. KhudaBukhsh ·
Guha Jayachandran

Low Resource Social Media Text Mining

 Springer

Shriphani Palakodety 🆔
Onai Inc.
San Jose, CA, USA

Guha Jayachandran
Onai Inc.
San Jose, CA, USA

Ashiqur R. KhudaBukhsh 🆔
Golisano College of Computing
and Information Sciences
Rochester Institute of Technology
Rochester, NY, USA

ISSN 2191-5768   ISSN 2191-5776 (electronic)
SpringerBriefs in Computer Science
ISBN 978-981-16-5624-8   ISBN 978-981-16-5625-5 (eBook)
https://doi.org/10.1007/978-981-16-5625-5

This Springer imprint is published by the registered company Springer Nature Singapore Pte Ltd.
The registered company address is: 152 Beach Road, #21-01/04 Gateway East, Singapore 189721, Singapore

To Sai, Ramani and Shrinivas Palakodety.

In memoriam Dr. Jaime Carbonell.

Preface

Most natural language processing work has been on world languages like English, but most people in the world speak other languages that are comparatively poorly resourced in terms of training data and research attention. Significant strides have been made recently in low-resource NLP research. Powerful unsupervised methods, large-scale multilingual language models, and other innovations have enabled rapid progress in a variety of areas for low-resource NLP. However, real world text analyses are rarely standalone tasks and practitioners often combine several methods. This book describes important advances in low-resource NLP and contains real world examples explaining how to assemble them to perform robust, sophisticated text analyses. Low-resource NLP is an important component of many text mining tasks including socially conscious applications of AI. This book will provide the insights and examples needed to perform such analyses rigorously.

San Jose, CA, USA Shriphani Palakodety
July 2021

Contents

Acronyms

NLP	Natural Language Processing
AI	Artificial Intelligence
LI	Language Identification
L1 Language	A person's first language
L2 Language	A person's second language—typically not the native language
SGD	Stochastic Gradient Descent
LDA	Latent Dirichlet Allocation
SVD	Singular Value Decomposition
COHA	Corpus Of Historical American English

Chapter 1
Introduction

Over recent years, rapid growth in internet access across the globe has resulted in an explosion in user-generated text content in social media platforms. This effect is significantly pronounced in linguistically diverse areas of the world like South Asia, where over 400 million people regularly access social media platforms. YouTube, WhatsApp, and Facebook, each report monthly active user bases in excess of 200 million from this region.[1,2,3] NLP research, and publicly available resources like models and corpora, prioritize web content authored primarily by a Western user base. Such content is authored in English by a user base fluent in the language and can be processed by a broad range of off-the-shelf NLP tools. In contrast, text from linguistically diverse regions features high levels of multilinguality, code mixing [5], and varied language skill levels [6]. Resources like corpora and models are also scarce. Due to these factors, newer methods are needed to process such text.

This book is designed for NLP practitioners well-versed in recent advances in the field but unfamiliar with the landscape of low-resource multilingual NLP. The contents of this book introduce the various challenges associated with social media content, quantify these issues, and provide solutions and intuition. Special focus is placed on methods that are unsupervised or require minimal supervision, vital in the low-resource domain. When possible, the methods discussed are evaluated on real-world social media data sets to emphasize their robustness to the noisy nature of the social media environment.

On completion of this book, the reader will be well-versed with the complexity of text-mining in multilingual, low-resource environments; will be aware of a broad set of off-the-shelf tools that can be applied to various problems; and will be able to conduct sophisticated analyses of such text.

The book is organized as follows. Chapter 2 introduces the low-resource, multilingual setting. We discuss the impact of varying language skill levels and how

---

[1] https://inc42.com/buzz/youtube-has-over-325-mn-monthly-users-in-india-gaming-rules/.

[2] https://techcrunch.com/2019/07/26/whatsapp-india-users-400-million/.

[3] https://www.livemint.com/Consumer/CyEKdaltF64YycZsU72oEK/Indians-largest-audience-country-for-Facebook-Report.html.

© The Author(s), under exclusive license to Springer Nature Singapore Pte Ltd. 2021   1
S. Palakodety et al., *Low Resource Social Media Text Mining*, SpringerBriefs
in Computer Science, https://doi.org/10.1007/978-981-16-5625-5_1

that is reflected in statistics like out-of-vocabulary rates, phenomena observed exclusively in multilingual communities like code mixing and Romanization. We quantify these phenomena in social media data sets and demonstrate why addressing these challenges is necessary for any well-formed analysis.

Chapter 3 provides a broad overview of NLP methods utilized in the rest of the book. We start with word embeddings, in particular the SkipGram model [3], sub-word extensions [1] and their remarkable success in noisy environments, and other variants. We cover transformer based language models including BERT [2] and GPT [4], and their uses in text-mining tasks. We then focus on NLP applications like machine translation and semantic sampling and discuss an emerging area of NLP, polyglot training, that has provided gains in a variety of multilingual settings.

Chapter 4 introduces the language identification task and the associated challenges with noisy, multilingual, code mixed social media text. We discuss how to formulate the language-identification problem, the various granularity levels involved, and unsupervised methods for this task.

Chapter 5 introduces recent breakthroughs in unsupervised machine translation, where bilingual dictionaries can be constructed with no parallel corpora. We provide an overview of the problem, explore how it can be utilized for other tasks like semantic and cross-lingual sampling, and provide insight into why these methods work.

Chapter 6 introduces the semantic sampling task, the task of retrieving content from an unlabeled document pool that is similar to an input query document. We cover a plethora of methods combining contextual embeddings, and word embeddings. We then explore the cross-lingual variant, where the input document and the unlabeled pool are authored in different languages. We explore the phenomenon of code mixing and how it can be applied for this task.

Where possible we provide case studies from published research that utilize real social media data. The topics included here have a wide variety of applications including content moderation, AI for social good (including detecting *hate speech* - an area of active research), recommendation engines, and many more.

For NLP practitioners accustomed to a primarily English-speaking user base and audience, this book introduces the NLP issues surrounding low resource languages and multilinguality, and provides a set of robust tools that can be composed to solve sophisticated data-mining and text-mining problems. Given the rapid growth of such content, and the comparative lack of NLP resources, the methods discussed in this book are of increasing importance.

References

1. Bojanowski P, Grave E, Joulin A, Mikolov T (2017) Enriching word vectors with subword information. Trans Assoc Compu Linguist 5:135–146
2. Devlin J, Chang MW, Lee K, Toutanova K (2019) BERT: pre-training of deep bidirectional transformers for language understanding. In: Proceedings of the 2019 conference of the North American Chapter of the Association for Computational Linguistics: Human Language Technologies,

vol 1 (Long and Short Papers). Association for Computational Linguistics, Minneapolis, pp 4171–4186. https://doi.org/10.18653/v1/N19-1423. https://aclanthology.org/N19-1423

3. Mikolov T, Sutskever I, Chen K, Corrado G, Dean J (2013) Distributed representations of words and phrases and their compositionality. In: Proceedings of the 26th international conference on neural information processing systems, vol 2. Curran Associates Inc., Red Hook, NIPS'13, pp 3111–3119

4. Radford A, Wu J, Child R, Luan D, Amodei D, Sutskever I (2019) Language models are unsupervised multitask learners

5. Rijhwani S, Sequiera R, Choudhury M, Bali K, Maddila CS (2017) Estimating code-switching on Twitter with a novel generalized word-level language detection technique. In: Proceedings of the 55th Annual Meeting of the Association for Computational Linguistics (Volume 1: Long Papers), Association for Computational Linguistics, Vancouver, pp 1971–1982. https://doi.org/10.18653/v1/P17-1180. https://aclanthology.org/P17-1180

6. Sarkar R, Mahinder S, KhudaBukhsh A (2020) The non-native speaker aspect: Indian English in social media. In: Proceedings of the Sixth Workshop on Noisy User-generated Text (W-NUT 2020), Association for Computational Linguistics, Online, pp 61–70. https://doi.org/10.18653/v1/2020.wnut-1.9. https://aclanthology.org/2020.wnut-1.9

Chapter 2
The Problem Setting

Abstract We first introduce the domain of this book: low resource social media text. The domain encompasses some of the most used languages in the world and a wide variety of tasks and applications. We explore the socio-technical conditions that lead to such text, and how it influences expression online. Examples and statistics are provided from various social media data sets and recent research. We then cover attempts to bridge the resource gap between world languages like English and low-resource languages. Special attention is given to the various data acquisition strategies employed by researchers. This chapter will help NLP practitioners understand the importance of analyzing the low-resource components of corpora from various societies and how ignoring them can skew results, how to go about addressing these, and a broad set of examples and statistics to reinforce the importance of low-resource social media text mining.

Keywords Low-resource NLP · Multilinguality · L1 language · L2 language · Language preference · Language and geography · Bilingualism

Low-resource NLP is concerned with NLP methods in domains where resources like corpora, annotations, and even annotators are limited or even non-existent.

At first glance it may seem that low-resource NLP is limited to rare or endangered languages but this is only a small sliver of low-resource NLP. Languages with hundreds of millions of speakers manifest in ways that can be considered low-resource settings. Resources such as corpora and models, often developed with a particular setting in mind, can be ill-suited to other domains. A variety of cultural, historical, and socio-technical factors can cause a highly-used language to be under-addressed by NLP research. Consider the example of Romanized-Hindi ("Hinglish"). Recent estimates [33] suggest that this is the dominant language on social media from India owing to factors like lack of high-quality input methods for non-Roman characters [5]. Yet, owing to its informal, non-standard nature, Romanized Hindi never appears in books, Wikipedia articles and other formal resources that are used to compile and construct large-scale NLP corpora. As a result, models developed for Hindi authored in the native Devanagari script do not work on Romanized Hindi, and this extremely popular medium of expression is thus poorly addressed by existing NLP research. Tasks considered trivial on formal, well-formed text often require serious attention when short, noisy texts like social media posts are used as input [7, 17, 29, 37]. Consider the task of conducting NLP on social media posts produced by displaced groups like refugees. In addition to the low-resource nature of the languages used by such communities, acquiring expert annotators can be nearly impossible. Low resource NLP tasks are thus shaped by the social, cultural, and economic backgrounds of the associated communities, by limitations in technology, and by the medium of expression.

In this book, we operate at the intersection of low-resource NLP and social media text. A variety of socio-linguistic phenomena appear in this setting, including multilinguality, and spelling and grammar disfluencies in content generated by non-native speakers among others. Due to rapidly increasing internet and social media penetration in many societies, a significant number of geopolitical events are discussed and shaped online. Developing methods for analyzing user-generated content from these communities thus has many direct applications in political analysis [31], in socially conscious applications of AI [8, 34, 36], and in estimating the evolution of language [33, 38].

The methods discussed in this text prioritize limited resource requirements—methods that directly operate on the data set and require minimal external resources like additional corpora, models, or annotations. Owing to this, these methods are easily transferable to many domains such as different language families, data sources, or applications.

We now elaborate on the various aspects of our setting, and why they need addressing.

2.1 Multilinguality

Multilingual societies are among the fastest growing online populations and are an ever increasing source of user-generated social media content. Users often utilize the full range of their language skills online—generating text content in multiple languages, often in the same short text boundary. Large scale corpus acquisition efforts from multilingual societies will almost always yield a multilingual corpus—and the languages included in the mix will inevitably include under-resourced languages and dialects.

In fact, even large urban metropolitan areas around the world are highly multilingual. For instance, an analysis of tweets from Manchester, United Kingdom [3] revealed extensive use of Arabic, Malay, Mandarin, and Japanese. In fact Arabic was the second most used language on Twitter in Manchester—in stark contrast to census information. Malay, which also features in the top 10 languages, is poorly resourced in comparison with the rest of the language set [45].

A large-scale analysis of Twitter data from Quebec province, Canada, Qatar, and Switzerland reveals interesting insights about multilingual societies [26]. The three geographical regions of focus are highly multilingual societies. Twitter users in Queubec include primarily English and French speakers; in Qatar, Arabic and English

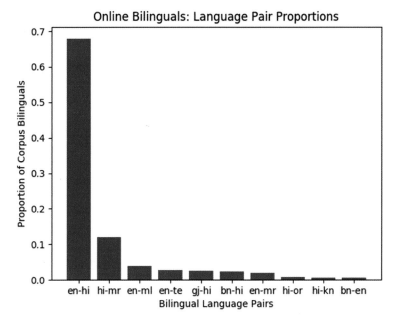

Fig. 2.1 Bilingual language-pair statistics on YouTube in India. A significant number of bilinguals use English and a native language.

speakers; in Switzerland English, German, French, Spanish, and Italian speakers. Large monolingual twitter user groups are observed and significant bilingual groups bridge these monolingual communities. In many cases, individual tweets contain a mix of several languages. Any social media analyses of these communities thus must include the full spectrum of language use including under resourced languages.

Estimates of language use in the Indian subcontinent on YouTube [33] reveal a significant presence of bilinguals that use English and a local language (Fig. 2.1). In almost all cases, the local languages are under-resourced despite their use by millions of speakers [21]. The study also reports a large presence of code mixed text where multiple languages appear in the same YouTube comment. Studies show that NLP models built with well-formed, monolingual text in mind are ill-suited for processing such text that abounds on social media platforms [23].

2.1.1 Romanization

Research to improve text input methods on mobile devices [5] often focuses on world languages like English. The quality and ease-of-use of text input methods for low-resource languages often lags far behind those for English. As a result, in many social media settings, we observe users eschew the native language script and use the Latin alphabet to author posts in their native language. Such Romanized text only occurs in informal settings like social media platforms. Large scale NLP resources are often constructed using formal sources like Wikipedia which is unlikely to include any Romanized variant and are thus unsuitable for processing such text.

In many cases, the Romanized variant is the preferred medium of expression among parts of the population. Arabic users who use Arabizi–Romanized Arabic—online consider it a *communication code* among their peers [1, 6] and use it extensively.

Studies on YouTube comments from the Indian subcontinent reveal extensive use of Romanization—to the point where the Romanized variants are the dominant form of native language expression online. In a collection of YouTube comments in response to videos posted by national news networks [34, 35], English, Romanized Hindi (Hinglish), and Hindi in the Devanagari script were observed and Hinglish was by far the most used form of expression. Figure 2.2 contains the language-specific breakdown of the corpus.

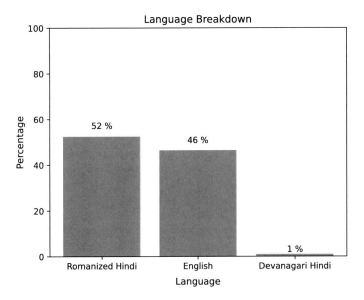

Fig. 2.2 Language breakdown in the Indian YouTube news comments corpus introduced by Palakodety et al. [34]. Note that Romanized Hindi is the dominant form of Hindi expression on social media and the native script is only present in trace amounts.

2.1.2 Geographic Spread

In large and geographically diverse populations, language use statistics only provide
a partial picture of the full language use. In an analysis by Palakodety et al. [33], we
notice that Romanized Hindi though dominant is only authored by a few provinces in
India. Figure 2.3 shows the extent of Hindi use and medium of expression through-
out India. Note that Hindi use is mostly concentrated in the Hindi belt states. In
fact, restricting analyses to Hindi only provides a geographically limited view. Any
analysis intended for the full geographic extent of India must thus incorporate each
of the dominant regional languages in these provinces, each of which manifest with
their own peculiarities such as distinct Romanization styles and diverse types of code
mixing. We also notice that limiting text analysis to a world language like English
can provide a skewed picture as well.

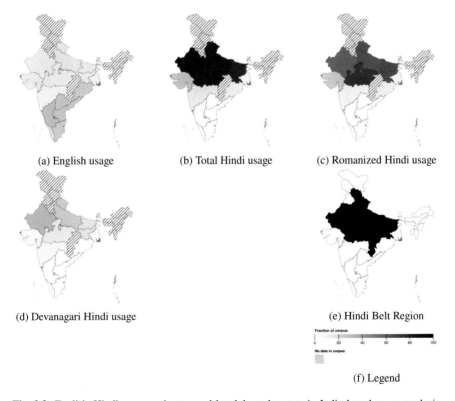

    (a) English usage   (b) Total Hindi usage   (c) Romanized Hindi usage

    (d) Devanagari Hindi usage   (e) Hindi Belt Region

                                               (f) Legend

Fig. 2.3 English–Hindi usage estimates and breakdown by state in India based on an analysis
by Palakodety et al. [33]. Note that Hindi use is concentrated in the Hindi belt. Also observe
that Romanized Hindi is the dominant form of Hindi expression on social media. The base maps
and geographic boundaries are from the Government of India and include disputed territories. No
opinions are intended on these matters

Additional analyses of social media content from the Indian subcontinent reveal high levels of code mixing, where multiple languages appear in the same short text boundary [4, 16, 33, 34]. In addition, the presence of close to 30 major languages in the region makes any large-scale annotation effort very difficult. NLP models that assume clean, well-formed, monolingual text are ill-suited for the type of user generated content on social media.

2.2 Disfluencies

Thus far, we have established that low-resource NLP methods are required due to the prevalence of poorly resourced and supported manifestations of popular languages on social media. However, even world languages like English can manifest in ways where existing resources can be rendered inadequate.

Consider that for the vast majority of the online population, English is at best an L2 language (a user's second language); most English users online are non-native speakers. English spelling in L2 speakers has been extensively studied [10, 27, 28, 46]. There is a large variation of English language skill levels online [41] and NLP tasks often require specialized methods when operating on English with a high-level of disfluencies [14, 15, 18, 23].

2.3 Language Influencing Semantics

A large body of work has been conducted to infer a variety of social and geopolitcal themes and signals from social media data. For instance, the relationship between tweets and opinion polls [31, 32], attribution of blame during a water shortage event in a major Indian metropolis [42], consumer opinions on brands [20], the extent of political polarization in the US [25] and many other topics have been studied through the lens of social media. Social media analysis is an important component of social science research.

However, most such analyses are complicated in multilingual societies. It is often observed that certain leanings or sentiments are overrepresented or underrepresented in a subset of the dominant languages in use. This effect is observed across a variety of topics. For instance, through a large scale analysis of tweets, Rudra et al. discovered that Hindi was the language of choice for *swearing, and expressing negative sentiment* [40], and English was the preferred medium of expression for *expressing positive sentiment*. Through a web questionnaire, Dewaele discovered that the L1 language i.e. an individual's first language, is the primary choice for expressing swearwords and taboo words [13]. On the other hand, KhudaBukhsh et al. showed that *hope speech*—speech designed to de-escalate conflict is substantially rarer in Hindi as opposed to English [24].

These results show us that the full nature of intersection of multilinguality and sentiment is yet to be discovered. Given, the ever increasing number of multilingual societies in many parts of the world, and the varied traditions and histories of the areas, it is increasingly clear that no comprehensive social media text analysis can be conducted without taking the multi-lingual (and low-resource languages) into account. In fact research that discards the low-resource components and solely focuses on well-resourced world languages like English or French, will capture only a small portion of the full picture. Low resource NLP is thus an important and required component of any serious social media text analysis.

2.4 Recent Efforts in Low Resource NLP

In recent years, NLP research has placed tremendous focus on curating and developing large-scale multilingual corpora and models. Transformer based models which are the state of the art in many NLP tasks [9, 12] are available for hundreds of languages and efforts in the NLP community are under way for increasing the coverage of such models [19, 44]. In recent years, significant awareness efforts are under way in the NLP community through publications [21], events [11, 43], and advocacy [39].

Methods designed for low-resource NLP are rarely isolated efforts. Recent evidence suggests that multilingual NLP models provide benefits even for well-resourced languages [2, 22, 30]. In the rest of this book, we provide a variety of methods and the associated background knowledge required to tackle a variety of low-resource social media text analyses.

References

1. Alsulami A (2019) A sociolinguistic analysis of the use of Arabizi in social media among Saudi Arabians. Int J English Linguist 9:257. https://doi.org/10.5539/ijel.v9n6p257
2. Artetxe M, Schwenk H (2019) Massively multilingual sentence embeddings for zero-shot cross-lingual transfer and beyond. Trans Assoc Comput Linguistics 7:597–610, https://transacl.org/ojs/index.php/tacl/article/view/1742
3. Bailey G, Goggins J, Ingham T (2013) What can twitter tell us about the language diversity of greater manchester? Technical report, School of Languages, Linguistics and Cultures, The University of Manchester, Manchester
4. Bali K, Sharma J, Choudhury M, Vyas Y (2014) I am borrowing ya mixing?" an analysis of English-Hindi code mixing in Facebook. In: Proceedings of the first workshop on computational approaches to code switching. Association for Computational Linguistics, Doha, pp 116–126. https://doi.org/10.3115/v1/W14-3914. https://aclanthology.org/W14-3914
5. Bi X, Smith BA, Zhai S (2012) Multilingual touchscreen keyboard design and optimization. Hum Comput Interact 27(4):352–382
6. Bou Tanios J (2016) Language choice and romanization online by Lebanese Arabic speakers. Universitat Pompeu Fabra, Barcelona, Technical report
7. Choudhury M, Bali K, Sitaram S, Baheti A (2017) Curriculum design for code-switching: experiments with language identification and language modeling with deep neural networks.

In: Proceedings of the 14th international conference on natural language processing (ICON-2017), NLP Association of India, Kolkata, pp 65–74. https://aclanthology.org/W17-7509
8. Chowdhury HA, Nibir TA, Islam MS (2018) Sentiment analysis of comments on rohingya movement with support vector machine. 1803.08790
9. Conneau A, Khandelwal K, Goyal N, Chaudhary V, Wenzek G, Guzmán F, Grave E, Ott M, Zettlemoyer L, Stoyanov V (2019) Unsupervised cross-lingual representation learning at scale. arXiv preprint arXiv:191102116
10. Cook V (1997) L2 users and English spelling. J Multilingual Multicult Dev 18(6):474–488
11. DeepLo-2019 (2021) Deep learning for low-resource NLP. https://sites.google.com/view/deeplo19
12. Devlin J, Chang MW, Lee K, Toutanova K (2019) BERT: Pre-training of deep bidirectional transformers for language understanding. In: Proceedings of the 2019 conference of the North American Chapter of the Association for Computational Linguistics: Human Language Technologies, vol 1 (Long and Short Papers). Association for Computational Linguistics, Minneapolis, pp 4171–4186. https://doi.org/10.18653/v1/N19-1423. https://aclanthology.org/N19-1423
13. Dewaele JM (2004) The emotional force of swearwords and taboo words in the speech of multilinguals. J Multilingual Multicult Dev 25:204–222. https://doi.org/10.1080/01434630408666529
14. Foster J, Vogel C (2004) Parsing ill-formed text using an error grammar. Artif Intell Rev 21:269–291. https://doi.org/10.1023/B:AIRE.0000036259.68818.1e
15. Foster J, Wagner J, van Genabith J (2008) Adapting a WSJ-trained parser to grammatically noisy text. In: Proceedings of ACL-08: HLT, Short Papers. Association for Computational Linguistics, Columbus, pp 221–224. https://aclanthology.org/P08-2056
16. Gella S, Bali K, Choudhury M (2014) "ye word kis lang ka hai bhai?" testing the limits of word level language identification. In: Proceedings of the 11th international conference on natural language processing. NLP Association of India, Goa, pp 368–377. https://aclanthology.org/W14-5151
17. Gimpel K, Schneider N, O'Connor B, Das D, Mills D, Eisenstein J, Heilman M, Yogatama D, Flanigan J, Smith NA (2011) Part-of-speech tagging for Twitter: annotation, features, and experiments. In: Proceedings of the 49th Annual Meeting of the Association for Computational Linguistics: Human Language Technologies. Association for Computational Linguistics, Portland, pp 42–47. https://aclanthology.org/P11-2008
18. Hashemi HB, Hwa R (2016) An evaluation of parser robustness for ungrammatical sentences. In: Proceedings of the 2016 conference on empirical methods in natural language processing. Association for Computational Linguistics, Austin, pp 1765–1774. https://doi.org/10.18653/v1/D16-1182. https://aclanthology.org/D16-1182
19. Hugging Face (2021) Hugging face: models. Hugging Face. https://huggingface.co/models
20. Jansen BJ, Zhang M, Sobel K, Chowdury A (2009) Twitter power: Tweets as electronic word of mouth. J Am Soc Inf Sci Technol 60(11):2169–2188
21. Joshi P, Santy S, Budhiraja A, Bali K, Choudhury M (2020) The state and fate of linguistic diversity and inclusion in the NLP world. In: Proceedings of the 58th Annual Meeting of the Association for Computational Linguistics. Association for Computational Linguistics, Online, pp 6282–6293. https://doi.org/10.18653/v1/2020.acl-main.560. https://aclanthology.org/2020.acl-main.560
22. Karthikeyan K, Wang Z, Mayhew S, Roth D (2020) Cross-lingual ability of multilingual BERT: an empirical study. In: Proceedings of the international conference on learning representations, https://cogcomp.seas.upenn.edu/papers/KWMR20.pdf
23. Khudabukhsh A, Palakodety S, Carbonell J (2020) On NLP methods robust to noisy Indian social media data. In: AI for Social Good Workshop
24. KhudaBukhsh AR, Palakodety S, Carbonell JG (2020) Harnessing code switching to transcend the linguistic barrier. In: Bessiere C (ed) Proceedings of the twenty-ninth international joint conference on artificial intelligence, IJCAI-20, International Joint Conferences on Artificial Intelligence Organization, pp 4366–4374, special track on AI for CompSust and Human well-being

25. KhudaBukhsh AR, Sarkar R, Kamlet M, Mitchell TM (2021) We don't speak the same language: interpreting polarization through machine translation. In: AAAI

26. Kim S, Weber I, Wei L, Oh A (2014) Sociolinguistic analysis of twitter in multilingual societies. In: Proceedings of the 25th ACM conference on hypertext and social media, Association for Computing Machinery, New York, HT '14, pp 243–248. https://doi.org/10.1145/2631775.2631824.

27. Liow SJR, Lau LHS (2006) The development of bilingual children's early spelling in english. J Educ Psychol 98(4):868

28. Maruthy S, Raj N, Geetha MP, Priya CS (2015) Disfluency characteristics of Kannada-English bilingual adults who stutter. J Commun Disorders 56:19–28

29. Mave D, Maharjan S, Solorio T (2018) Language identification and analysis of code-switched social media text. In: Proceedings of the third workshop on computational approaches to linguistic code-switching. Association for Computational Linguistics, Melbourne, pp 51–61. https://doi.org/10.18653/v1/W18-3206. https://aclanthology.org/W18-3206

30. Mulcaire P, Kasai J, Smith NA (2019) Polyglot contextual representations improve crosslingual transfer. In: Proceedings of the 2019 conference of the North American Chapter of the Association for Computational Linguistics: human language technologies, vol 1 (Long and Short Papers). Association for Computational Linguistics, Minneapolis, pp 3912–3918. https://doi.org/10.18653/v1/N19-1392. https://www.aclweb.org/anthology/N19-1392

31. O'Connor B, Balasubramanyan R, Routledge B, Smith N (2010) From tweets to polls: linking text sentiment to public opinion time series. In: Proceedings of the international AAAI conference on web and social media 4(1):122–129. https://ojs.aaai.org/index.php/ICWSM/article/view/14031

32. O'Connor BT (2018) Statistical text analysis for social science. https://doi.org/10.1184/R1/6723179.v1

33. Palakodety S, KhudaBukhsh A (2020) Annotation efficient language identification from weak labels. In: Proceedings of the sixth workshop on noisy user-generated text (W-NUT 2020). Association for Computational Linguistics, Online, pp 181–192. https://doi.org/10.18653/v1/2020.wnut-1.24. https://www.aclweb.org/anthology/2020.wnut-1.24

34. Palakodety S, KhudaBukhsh AR, Carbonell JG (2020a) Hope speech detection: a computational analysis of the voice of peace. In: Giacomo GD, Catalá A, Dilkina B, Milano M, Barro S, Bugarín A, Lang J (eds) ECAI 2020—24th European conference on artificial intelligence. Frontiers in Artificial Intelligence and Applications. IOS Press, vol 325, pp 1881–1889. https://doi.org/10.3233/FAIA200305.

35. Palakodety S, KhudaBukhsh AR, Carbonell JG (2020b) Mining insights from large-scale corpora using fine-tuned language models. In: Giacomo GD, Catalá A, Dilkina B, Milano M, Barro S, Bugarín A, Lang J (eds) ECAI 2020—24th European conference on artificial intelligence, 29 Aug–8 Sept 2020, Santiago de Compostela, Spain, Aug 29–Sept 8 2020—Including 10th conference on prestigious applications of artificial intelligence (PAIS 2020). Frontiers in artificial intelligence and applications. IOS Press, vol 325, pp 1890–1897. https://doi.org/10.3233/FAIA200306.

36. Palakodety S, KhudaBukhsh AR, Carbonell JG (2020c) Voice for the voiceless: active sampling to detect comments supporting the Rohingyas. In: Proceedings of the AAAI conference on artificial intelligence, vol 34(01), pp 454–462

37. Patro J, Samanta B, Singh S, Basu A, Mukherjee P, Choudhury M, Mukherjee A (2017) All that is English may be Hindi: enhancing language identification through automatic ranking of the likeliness of word borrowing in social media. In: Proceedings of the 2017 conference on empirical methods in natural language processing. Association for Computational Linguistics, Copenhagen, pp 2264–2274. https://doi.org/10.18653/v1/D17-1240. https://aclanthology.org/D17-1240

38. Rijhwani S, Sequiera R, Choudhury M, Bali K, Maddila CS (2017) Estimating code-switching on Twitter with a novel generalized word-level language detection technique. In: Proceedings of the 55th Annual Meeting of the Association for Computational Linguistics, vol 1: Long

Papers. Association for Computational Linguistics, Vancouver, pp 1971–1982. https://doi.org/10.18653/v1/P17-1180. https://aclanthology.org/P17-1180

39. Ruder S (2020) Why you should do NLP beyond English. Sebastian Ruder https://ruder.io/nlp-beyond-english/

40. Rudra K, Rijhwani S, Begum R, Bali K, Choudhury M, Ganguly N (2016) Understanding language preference for expression of opinion and sentiment: what do Hindi-English speakers do on Twitter? In: Proceedings of the 2016 conference on empirical methods in natural language processing. Association for Computational Linguistics, Austin, pp 1131–1141. https://doi.org/10.18653/v1/D16-1121. https://www.aclweb.org/anthology/D16-1121

41. Sarkar R, Mahinder S, KhudaBukhsh A (2020) The non-native speaker aspect: Indian English in social media. In: Proceedings of the sixth workshop on noisy user-generated text (W-NUT 2020). Association for Computational Linguistics, Online, pp 61–70. https://doi.org/10.18653/v1/2020.wnut-1.9. https://aclanthology.org/2020.wnut-1.9

42. Sarkar R, Mahinder S, Sarkar H, KhudaBukhsh A (2020) Social media attributions in the context of water crisis. In: Proceedings of the 2020 conference on empirical methods in natural language processing (EMNLP). Association for Computational Linguistics, Online, pp 1402–1412. https://doi.org/10.18653/v1/2020.emnlp-main.109. https://www.aclweb.org/anthology/2020.emnlp-main.109

43. WiNLP (2021) Widening natural language processing. Widening Nat Lang Process. http://www.winlp.org/

44. XTREME (2021) Xtreme: (x) cross-lingual transfer evaluation of multilingual encoders. XTREME https://sites.research.google/xtreme

45. Yeong YL, Tan TP, Mohammad S (2016) Using dictionary and Lemmatizer to improve low resource English-Malay statistical machine translation system. Procedia Comput Sci 81:243–249. https://doi.org/10.1016/j.procs.2016.04.056

46. Yu J, Zhang L, Wu S, Zhang B (2017) Rhythm and disfluency: interactions in Chinese l2 English speech. In: 2017 20th Conference of the oriental chapter of the International Coordinating Committee on Speech Databases and Speech I/O Systems and Assessment (O-COCOSDA), IEEE, pp 1–6

Chapter 3
A Rapid Tour of NLP

Abstract In this chapter, we briefly review the NLP methods utilized in this book. Should the readers desire, a number of highly regarded texts have been authored recently (Eisenstein in Adaptive computation and machine learning series. MIT Press (2019) [9], Goldberg in Synth Lect Human Lang Technol 10(1):1-309 (2017) [11]) which provide a thorough and rigorous grounding of NLP. We discuss static and contextual word and document embeddings, and their applications. We then look at polyglot training in static and contextual embeddings.

Keywords Word embeddings · Document embeddings · BERT language model · GPT · SkipGram embeddings · FastText embeddings · Polyglot training

3.1 Embeddings

Almost all the methods we discuss in this book involve constructing and reasoning about continuous, dense vector representations of words and documents—called *embeddings*. In a social media context, a document is typically a tweet, a social media post or any other short text unit. Vector representations allow us to reason about words, documents, and corpora using the tools of coordinate geometry.

3.1.1 Word Embeddings

We first discuss static word embeddings—where a word is given a single, fixed, vector.

3.1.1.1 SkipGram Embeddings

The method of most interest to us is the SkipGram model introduced by Mikolov et al. [24, 25]. The SkipGram model is a form of *self-supervised learning*. The model takes a word as input, and predicts the word's context. The model is parameterized by a collection of dense vectors—one per word—the word embeddings.

© The Author(s), under exclusive license to Springer Nature Singapore Pte Ltd. 2021   15
S. Palakodety et al., *Low Resource Social Media Text Mining*, SpringerBriefs
in Computer Science, https://doi.org/10.1007/978-981-16-5625-5_3

Given an input word w, the model predicts words in the context (a small window) of w. Given, words w, and c, the probability that c occurs in the context of w is given by Eq. 3.1.

$$s(c, w) = \sigma(\text{emb}(c) \cdot \text{emb}(w)) \tag{3.1}$$

where σ is the sigmoid function, and $\text{emb}(x)$ returns the embedding of word x. The inverse probability—that c does not occur in w's context is given by Eq. 3.2.

$$s'(c, w) = \sigma(-\text{emb}(c) \cdot \text{emb}(w)) \tag{3.2}$$

The model is provided a set of word pairs sourced from the corpus. Word pairs that occur in the same context are the positives and synthetic negative examples include words that do not occur in the same context in the corpus (this is referred to as negative sampling). At training time, for each positive pair (c_+, w) sourced from the corpus, a set of K negative pairs is sampled: (c_{k-}, w).

The loss function for the model is:

$$\mathcal{L} = -\left[\log s(c_+, w) + \sum_{k=1}^{K} \log s'(c_{k-}, w) \right] \tag{3.3}$$

where:

$\log s(c_+, w)$ log likelihood that c_+ occurs in w's context
$\log s'(c_{k-}, w)$ log likelihood that c_{k-} *does not occur* in w's context

Thus the loss function $\mathcal{L}$ maximizes the log likelihood that the positive example c_+ occurs in w's context, and maximizes the log likelihood that the negative example c_{k-} *does not occur* in w's context.

The model is trained using stochastic gradient descent. An illustration is provided in Fig. 3.1.

SkipGram word vectors are just one of several types of static embeddings that are widely used in NLP tasks. GloVe vectors [35] are trained with a slightly different objective than SkipGram embeddings—the inner product of two embeddings should return the log probability of their co-occurrence in a short context window. The continuous bag-of-words model (CBOW) [24] combines (by averaging) the embeddings of a set of context words, and predicts the word in the middle (i.e. inverts the SkipGram training objective).

3.1.2   Sub-word Extensions

Recall Chap. 2 where we showed the high level of spelling disfluencies. Consider the word where and its misspelled variant whre. Ideally, we would like the misspelled

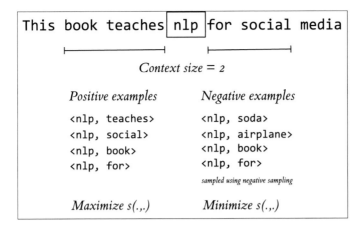

Fig. 3.1 The SkipGram pipeline for a single document. For the word `nlp` in the document `This book teaches nlp for social media`, we obtain positive examples, obtain negative examples from the corpus (using negative sampling) and maximize the score $s(.,.)$ defined in Eq. 3.1

variant to have an embedding close to the correct version. Obtaining representations robust to noise that is typical of social media is critical for a variety of analyses. Bojanowski et al. [3] introduced an extension to the SkipGram model that represents a word's embedding as a sum of the constituent character n-gram embeddings. For example, the word `where` contains the character 3-grams: `[whe, her, ere]`, and the character 4-grams: `[wher, here]`. Each of these *n*-grams is assigned an embedding which is trained during the training phase. The word `where` itself is assigned the embedding obtained by adding together all the constituent character *n*-gram embeddings. These sub-word representations are shared across all the words and thus robust embeddings can be obtained even in the presence of misspellings. In practice, all character *n*-grams are included for $n \geq 3$ and $n \leq 6$.

We refer to the 100-dimensional word embeddings trained with this sub-word extension as `FastText-100` in this book.

3.1.3 Document Embeddings

Analogous to word embeddings, document embeddings assign a vector to a document. In the social media context, a document is typically a social media post like a tweet, or a comment. Document embeddings have been used in almost all areas of NLP. In the vector space model in information retrieval [38], documents and queries are represented as vectors and a vector similarity metric is used as a measure of relevance. In topic modeling [2, 15], a document is represented as a vector of proportions of latent topics.

Of most interest to us in this book are dense document embeddings constructed in a similar fashion to word embeddings.

A common and highly successful technique is treating a document as a *bag of words* and obtaining its embedding by merely averaging the constituent word embeddings. Simply averaging a document's constituent word embeddings is a powerful technique that is competitive with far more sophisticated models [17, 47]. More advanced variants can compute a weighted average [1] of the constituent word embeddings. `sent2vec` embeddings [31] extend the `FastText-100` embeddings discussed above to documents.

3.1.4   Applications

Static word and document embeddings have been applied to almost every NLP task. In keeping with the theme of the book, we cover some applications of word embeddings to analyze social media data.

Biases in Word Embeddings: Can word embeddings be used to quantify and study biases and stereotypes towards women, and ethnic minorities? Garg et al. [10] trained word embeddings on various corpora including news items [24, 25], books, and a corpus of historical American English (COHA) [14]. Word lists were created to represent male and female genders, ethnicities, and occupations and adjectives. For instance, men were represented by the word list [he, son, his, him, father, man, boy, himself, ...], and one such word list per gender, ethnicity, and religion were constructed. To quantify bias, the average distance from a word list to an occupation or adjective were computed and the difference between the average distances for men and women (i.e. their word lists)—a negative result meant stronger association with men and a positive result meant stronger association with women. Results showed that the embeddings associated *women* with occupations like *nurse, librarian, secretary* more than with *carpenter, engineer, mechanic*. Ethnic stereotypes were also encoded in the embeddings. For instance, *hispanic* was associated with *housekeeper, mason, artist, janitor*, versus *asian* with *professor, official, secretary*. Temporal analyses included the evolution of such bias and associations over the past century.

Political Polarization in Social Media: What are the linguistic aspects of political polarization on social media. Demszky et al. [6] proposed a topic modeling framework for quantifying the linguistic dimensions of political polarization on a data set of 4m tweets on 21 mass shootings. GloVe vectors were trained on the full corpus and document embeddings were obtained for a sample of tweets using the method proposed by Arora et al. [1]. These embeddings were clustered using k-Means clustering and the resulting tweet clusters—the *topics*—inspected. For the topics involved, a partisanship estimate revealed the various linguistic facets of political polarization. For example, tweets expressing *solidarity* were among the *least polarized*. In contrast, tweets expressing the *shooter's identity* and *ideology* were *highly polarized*.

The method showed that topics discovered by GloVe vectors were superior to those obtained using traditional methods like LDA [2]—both in the grouping and cohesion of the topics.

Domain-Specific Sentiment Lexicons: Different terms carry different meanings in various settings. For instance, *soft* carries a negative connotation in sport, but a positive connotation in say bedding. Hamilton et al. [13] introduced the SENTPROP framework, to automatically assign positive and negative attributes to words in a corpus using SVD-based word embeddings, and a small seed set containing initial positive and negative polarities. The method discovers polarities (positive or negative) and a score indicating the extent of polarity. Experiments show that on a corpus of social media posts on various sub-reddits on the website Reddit,[1] words like *difficult* are *positive* in the sports community[2] and negative in the women-focused community.[3] On the COHA corpus [14], *lean* went from *negative to positive* during the period from 1860 to 1980, referring to *muscular* recently instead of *weak* in 1860. The word *pathetic* went from *positive to negative* in the same period, referring to *weak* recently and *passionate* in 1860. The same method was applied to FastText-100 embeddings trained on a corpus of YouTube comments relevant to the Rohingya refugee crisis [34] revealing the predominantly negative view on social media towards the Rohingya refugee community.

In addition to these tasks, analogy tasks on word embeddings were used to uncover mental health biases in various communities [41], and investigate racial biases [22]. We reinforce that these are only a select few applications of static embeddings to the analysis of social media text out of a very thriving and active body of work [30].

3.2 Contextual Embeddings

In contrast to static or fixed word embeddings, contextual word embeddings vary based on the context in which they appear. Contextual embeddings and models that yield contextual embeddings [20] are the state-of-the-art for many NLP tasks [18, 44].

3.2.1 BERT

BERT [7] models text as a sequence of tokens. Two training objectives are utilized. First, in the input sequence, a few of the tokens are masked and the model has to predict these tokens. Next, given two sentences, the model predicts if the second

---

[1] https://reddit.com.

[2] https://reddit.com/r/sports.

[3] https://reddit.com/r/TwoX.

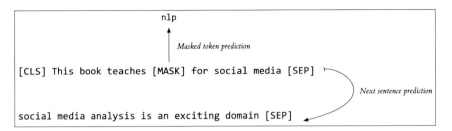

Fig. 3.2 The BERT pipeline

follows the first. Two special tokens are introduced: [CLS] is always the first token in the input, and [SEP] separates sentences. A transformer encoder [43] forms the backbone. An illustration is presented in Fig. 3.2.

A variety of pre-trained BERT models are available (varying typically in training corpus, model size, casing, and language) [16]. The typical downstream application takes a pre-trained BERT model, adds a custom task-specific output layer, and fine-tunes it [7, 8]. Alternately, representations for the [CLS] token are used directly as a document representation [48], or the representations for all the tokens are averaged and used as a document embedding.

3.2.2   GPT

The GPT family of models [4, 36, 37] are large scale language models which predict the next token given k previous tokens and incorporate the transformer architecture [25]. GPT-3, the latest incarnation [4], in particular has received significant attention due to applications in high-quality text generation, few-shot question-answering, and more.

3.2.3   Applications

Social Bias Frames: Bias in statements like "*We shouldn't lower our standards to hire more women*" contains the implication that women (the target of the statement) are less qualified. Sap et al. [39] utilized the GPT language model to predict whether such statements *intended to offend*, were *lewd*, or were *offensive*, the *target* of the statement, and the *implication*. Modeling the offensiveness, lewdness, and intention as categorical variables, and the targets and implications as free-text answers, a large data set was compiled. The GPT model was then shown the statement, the categorical variables and the free-text answers as a sequence of tokens at training time. For inference, given a statement, the trained model was asked to generate text that included the categorical variables and free-text answers. Results show that when the statement had a large lexical overlap with the free text answers, the model's predictions were very accurate.

Detecting *Hate Speech*: Mozafari et al. [26] mitigated data sparsity issues for detecting *hate speech* on social media using a variety of fine-tuning strategies obtaining a state-of-the-art result on various *hate speech* data sets.

Political Social Media Message Classification: Gupta et al. [12] used a fine-tuned BERT model to classify social media posts by political candidates during the 2016 US Presidential Election into various categories: *advocacy, attack, image, issue, call to action, ceremonial.*

Uncovering the National Mood: Can language models be used to discover the national mood surrounding various issues? Palakodety et al. [33] fine-tuned BERT on a large Indian social media corpus of YouTube comments on news videos. Questions were formulated as cloze statements [42] such as `[[CLS] India's biggest problem is [MASK] . [SEP]]` and predictions were collected for the masked token from the fine-tuned BERT model. Results showed that the model was capable of capturing the national mood around a variety of questions. Cloze statements such as `[[CLS] [MASK] will win . [SEP]]` were used to compute election forecasts and the results aligned with contemporaneous opinion polling.

3.3 Visualization

Due to the high dimensionality of the embedding spaces in question, it is often useful to visualize embeddings in two dimensions. Visualizations of embeddings have enabled discovery of several phenomena in deep learning and NLP [19, 32].

We discuss two techniques that are widely used in visualizing collections of embeddings. Robust software packages are widely available for these methods. "t-SNE" [21] is a popular dimension-reduction technique used to visualize embeddings. It is designed to preserve local similarities between data points while reducing the dimensionality of the data set. t-SNE is sensitive to the choice of hyper-parameters and care must be exercised while interpreting its results [46]. Recently, UMAP [23] has been proposed as an alternative to t-SNE. UMAP boasts a significantly faster runtime and preserves global structure better than t-SNE.

3.4   Polyglot Training

We dedicate a small section to polyglot training. In this scheme, a single NLP model is trained on a multilingual corpus. Polyglot variants of both static and contextual embeddings are used for a variety of tasks. Polyglot static embeddings have been utilized for unsupervised language identification [32, 34], and semantic role labeling [27].

In the contextual setting, the polyglot training scheme has been used to train large language models like the multilingual BERT (mBERT) [7], XLM-R [5], and Rosita [28]. Results show that these models are extremely effective for transfering resources from highly resourced languages to their poorly resourced counterparts. For instance, mBERT was used to transfer resources from English to 35 other languages across a wide range of tasks like natural language inference, document classification, named entity recognition, part-of-speech tagging, and dependency parsing. The resulting models were on par with or better than the state-of-the-art. Efforts to use mBERT to transfer resources to low resource languages and dialects like Arabizi [29], support entirely unseen low-resource languages [45], and transfer neural ranking models across languages [40] show significant promise.

References

1. Arora S, Liang Y, Ma T (2017) A simple but tough-to-beat baseline for sentence embeddings. In: ICLR
2. Blei DM, Ng AY, Jordan MI (2003) Latent Dirichlet allocation. J Mach Learn Res 3:993–1022
3. Bojanowski P, Grave E, Joulin A, Mikolov T (2017) Enriching word vectors with subword information. Trans Assoc Comput Linguis 5:135–146
4. Brown T, Mann B, Ryder N, Subbiah M, Kaplan JD, Dhariwal P, Neelakantan A, Shyam P, Sastry G, Askell A, Agarwal S, Herbert-Voss A, Krueger G, Henighan T, Child R, Ramesh A, Ziegler D, Wu J, Winter C, Hesse C, Chen M, Sigler E, Litwin M, Gray S, Chess B, Clark J, Berner C, McCandlish S, Radford A, Sutskever I, Amodei D (2020) Language models are few-shot learners. In: Larochelle H, Ranzato M, Hadsell R, Balcan MF, Lin H (eds) Advances in neural information processing systems. vol 33, pp 1877–1901. Curran Associates, Inc. https://proceedings.neurips.cc/paper/2020/file/1457c0d6bfcb4967418bfb8ac142f64a-Paper.pdf
5. Conneau A, Khandelwal K, Goyal N, Chaudhary V, Wenzek G, Guzmán F, Grave E, Ott M, Zettlemoyer L, Stoyanov V (2019) Unsupervised cross-lingual representation learning at scale. arXiv preprint arXiv:191102116
6. Demszky D, Garg N, Voigt R, Zou J, Shapiro J, Gentzkow M, Jurafsky D (2019) Analyzing polarization in social media: Method and application to tweets on 21 mass shootings. In: Proceedings of the 2019 conference of the North American Chapter of the Association for Computational Linguistics: Human Language Technologies, vol 1 (Long and Short Papers), Association for Computational Linguistics, Minneapolis, pp 2970–3005. https://doi.org/10.18653/v1/N19-1304. https://aclanthology.org/N19-1304
7. Devlin J, Chang MW, Lee K, Toutanova K (2019) BERT: Pre-training of deep bidirectional transformers for language understanding. In: Proceedings of the 2019 conference of the North American Chapter of the Association for Computational Linguistics: Human Language Technologies, vol 1 (Long and Short Papers), Association for Computational Linguistics, Minneapolis, pp 4171–4186. https://doi.org/10.18653/v1/N19-1423. https://aclanthology.org/N19-1423

8. Dodge J, Ilharco G, Schwartz R, Farhadi A, Hajishirzi H, Smith NA (2020) Fine-tuning pretrained language models: weight initializations, data orders, and early stopping. ArXiv abs/2002.06305

9. Eisenstein J (2019) Introduction to natural language processing. Adaptive computation and machine learning series. MIT Press. https://books.google.com/books?id=72yuDwAAQBAJ

10. Garg N, Schiebinger L, Jurafsky D, Zou J (2018) Word embeddings quantify 100 years of gender and ethnic stereotypes. In: Proceedings of the National Academy of Sciences, vol 115(16), pp E3635–E3644

11. Goldberg Y (2017) Neural network methods for natural language processing. Synth Lect Human Lang Technol 10(1):1–309

12. Gupta S, Bolden S, Kachhadia J, Korsunska A, Stromer-Galley J (2020) Polibert: classifying political social media messages with Bert. In: Social, cultural and behavioral modeling (SBP-BRIMS 2020) conference. Washington, DC

13. Hamilton WL, Clark K, Leskovec J, Jurafsky D (2016a) Inducing domain-specific sentiment lexicons from unlabeled corpora. In: Proceedings of the 2016 conference on empirical methods in natural language processing. Association for Computational Linguistics, Austin, pp 595–605. https://doi.org/10.18653/v1/D16-1057. https://aclanthology.org/D16-1057

14. Hamilton WL, Leskovec J, Jurafsky D (2016b) Diachronic word embeddings reveal statistical laws of semantic change. In: Proceedings of the 54th Annual Meeting of the Association for Computational Linguistics, vol 1: Long Papers. Association for Computational Linguistics, Berlin, pp 1489–1501. https://doi.org/10.18653/v1/P16-1141. https://aclanthology.org/P16-1141

15. Hofmann T (1999) Probabilistic latent semantic analysis. In: Proceedings of uncertainty in artificial intelligence, UAI'99, Stockholm. http://citeseer.ist.psu.edu/hofmann99probabilistic.html

16. Hugging Face (2021) Hugging face: pretrained models. Hugging Face. https://huggingface.co/transformers/pretrained_models.html

17. Iyyer M, Manjunatha V, Boyd-Graber J, Daumé III H (2015) Deep unordered composition rivals syntactic methods for text classification. In: Proceedings of the 53rd Annual Meeting of the Association for Computational Linguistics and the 7th International Joint Conference on Natural Language Processing, vo 1: Long Papers. Association for Computational Linguistics, Beijing, China, pp 1681–1691. https://doi.org/10.3115/v1/P15-1162. https://www.aclweb.org/anthology/P15-1162

18. Kakwani D, Kunchukuttan A, Golla S, NC G, Bhattacharyya A, Khapra MM, Kumar P (2020) IndicNLPSuite: monolingual corpora, evaluation benchmarks and pre-trained multilingual language models for Indian languages. In: Findings of the Association for Computational Linguistics: EMNLP 2020, Association for Computational Linguistics, Online, pp 4948–4961. https://doi.org/10.18653/v1/2020.findings-emnlp.445. https://aclanthology.org/2020.findings-emnlp.445

19. KhudaBukhsh AR, Palakodety S, Mitchell TM (2020) Discovering bilingual lexicons in polyglot word embeddings. CoRR abs/2008.13347. https://arxiv.org/abs/2008.13347, 2008.13347

20. Liu Q, Kusner MJ, Blunsom P (2020) A survey on contextual embeddings. ArXiv abs/2003.07278

21. Lvd Maaten, Hinton G (2008) Visualizing data using t-SNE. JMLR 9:2579–2605

22. Manzini T, Yao Chong L, Black AW, Tsvetkov Y (2019) Black is to criminal as Caucasian is to police: detecting and removing multiclass bias in word embeddings. In: Proceedings of the 2019 conference of the North American Chapter of the Association for Computational Linguistics: Human Language Technologies, vol 1 (Long and Short Papers). Association for Computational Linguistics, Minneapolis, pp 615–621. https://doi.org/10.18653/v1/N19-1062. https://aclanthology.org/N19-1062

23. McInnes L, Healy J, Saul N, Grossberger L (2018) UMAP: Uniform manifold approximation and projection. J Open Sour Softw 3(29):861

24. Mikolov T, Chen K, Corrado GS, Dean J (2013) Efficient estimation of word representations in vector space. http://arxiv.org/abs/1301.3781

25. Mikolov T, Sutskever I, Chen K, Corrado G, Dean J (2013b) Distributed representations of words and phrases and their compositionality. In: Proceedings of the 26th international conference on neural information processing systems, vol 2. Curran Associates Inc., Red Hook, NIPS'13, pp 3111–3119

26. Mozafari M, Farahbakhsh R, Crespi N (2020) A bert-based transfer learning approach for hate speech detection in online social media. In: Cherifi H, Gaito S, Mendes JF, Moro E, Rocha LM (eds) Complex networks and their applications VIII. Springer International Publishing, Cham, pp 928–940

27. Mulcaire P, Swayamdipta S, Smith NA (2018) Polyglot semantic role labeling. In: Proceedings of the 56th Annual Meeting of the Association for Computational Linguistics, vol 2: Short Papers. Association for Computational Linguistics, Melbourne, pp 667–672. https://doi.org/10.18653/v1/P18-2106. https://aclanthology.org/P18-2106

28. Mulcaire P, Kasai J, Smith NA (2019) Polyglot contextual representations improve crosslingual transfer. In: Proceedings of the 2019 conference of the North American Chapter of the Association for Computational Linguistics: Human Language Technologies, vol 1 (Long and Short Papers), Association for Computational Linguistics, Minneapolis, pp 3912–3918. https://doi.org/10.18653/v1/N19-1392. https://www.aclweb.org/anthology/N19-1392

29. Muller B, Sagot B, Seddah D (2020) Can multilingual language models transfer to an unseen dialect? A case study on north African Arabizi. ArXiv abs/2005.00318

30. NLP+CSS (2016) Natural language processing and computational social science. https://sites.google.com/site/nlpandcss/

31. Pagliardini M, Gupta P, Jaggi M (2018) Unsupervised learning of sentence embeddings using compositional n-Gram features. In: NAACL 2018—Conference of the North American Chapter of the Association for Computational Linguistics

32. Palakodety S, KhudaBukhsh AR, Carbonell JG (2020a) Hope speech detection: a computational analysis of the voice of peace. In: Giacomo GD, Catalá A, Dilkina B, Milano M, Barro S, Bugarín A, Lang J (eds) ECAI 2020—24th European Conference on Artificial Intelligence. Frontiers in Artificial intelligence and applications, vol 325. IOS Press, pp 1881–1889. https://doi.org/10.3233/FAIA200305.

33. Palakodety S, KhudaBukhsh AR, Carbonell JG (2020b) Mining insights from large-scale corpora using fine-tuned language models. In: Giacomo GD, Catalá A, Dilkina B, Milano M, Barro S, Bugarín A, Lang J (eds) ECAI 2020—24th European conference on Artificial Intelligence, 29 August-8 September 2020, Santiago de Compostela, Spain, August 29–September 8, 2020—Including 10th Conference on Prestigious Applications of Artificial Intelligence (PAIS 2020). Frontiers in artificial intelligence and applications. IOS Press, vol 325, pp 1890–1897. https://doi.org/10.3233/FAIA200306.

34. Palakodety S, KhudaBukhsh AR, Carbonell JG (2020c) Voice for the voiceless: active sampling to detect comments supporting the Rohingyas. In: Proceedings of the AAAI Conference on Artificial Intelligence, vol 34(01), pp 454–462

35. Pennington J, Socher R, Manning CD (2014) Glove: global vectors for word representation. In: Empirical methods in natural language processing (EMNLP), pp 1532–1543. http://www.aclweb.org/anthology/D14-1162

36. Radford A, Narasimhan K (2018) Improving language understanding by generative pre-training

37. Radford A, Wu J, Child R, Luan D, Amodei D, Sutskever I (2019) Language models are unsupervised multitask learners

38. Salton G, Wong A, Yang CS (1975) A vector space model for automatic indexing. Commun ACM 18(11):613–620

39. Sap M, Gabriel S, Qin L, Jurafsky D, Smith NA, Choi Y (2020) Social bias frames: reasoning about social and power implications of language. In: Proceedings of the 58th Annual Meeting of the Association for Computational Linguistics, Association for Computational Linguistics, Online, pp 5477–5490. https://doi.org/10.18653/v1/2020.acl-main.486. https://aclanthology.org/2020.acl-main.486

40. Shi P, Bai H, Lin J (2020) Cross-lingual training of neural models for document ranking. In: Findings of the Association for Computational Linguistics: EMNLP 2020, Association for

Computational Linguistics, Online, pp 2768–2773. https://doi.org/10.18653/v1/2020.findings-emnlp.249. https://aclanthology.org/2020.findings-emnlp.249

41. Straw I, Callison-Burch C (2020) Artificial intelligence in mental health and the biases of language based models. PLoS ONE 15. https://doi.org/10.1371/journal.pone.0240376

42. Taylor WL (1953) "Cloze procedure": a new tool for measuring readability. J Q 30(4):415–433. https://doi.org/10.1177/107769905303000401.

43. Vaswani A, Shazeer N, Parmar N, Uszkoreit J, Jones L, Gomez AN, Kaiser u, Polosukhin I (2017) Attention is all you need. In: Proceedings of the 31st international conference on neural information processing systems. Curran Associates Inc., Red Hook, NY, USA, NIPS'17, pp 6000–6010

44. Wang A, Singh A, Michael J, Hill F, Levy O, Bowman S (2018) GLUE: a multi-task benchmark and analysis platform for natural language understanding. In: Proceedings of the 2018 EMNLP Workshop BlackboxNLP: analyzing and interpreting neural networks for NLP. Association for Computational Linguistics, Brussels, Belgium, pp 353–355. DOIurl10.18653/v1/W18-5446. https://aclanthology.org/W18-5446

45. Wang Z, Karthikeyan K, Mayhew S, Roth D (2020) Extending multilingual BERT to low-resource languages. In: Findings of the association for computational linguistics: EMNLP 2020. Association for Computational Linguistics, Online, pp 2649–2656. https://doi.org/10.18653/v1/2020.findings-emnlp.240. https://aclanthology.org/2020.findings-emnlp.240

46. Wattenberg M, Viégas F, Johnson I (2016) How to use t-SNE effectively. Distill

47. Wieting J, Bansal M, Gimpel K, Livescu K (2016) Towards universal paraphrastic sentence embeddings. In: Bengio Y, LeCun Y (eds) 4th International conference on learning representations, ICLR 2016, San Juan, Puerto Rico, 2–4, 2016, Conference track proceedings. http://arxiv.org/abs/1511.08198

48. Yates A, Nogueira R, Lin J (2021) Pretrained transformers for text ranking: Bert and beyond. In: Proceedings of the 14th ACM international conference on web search and data mining, Association for Computing Machinery, New York, WSDM '21, pp 1154–1156. https://doi.org/10.1145/3437963.3441667

Chapter 4
Language Identification

Abstract We introduce the language identification problem—a vital component in a multilingual text analysis pipeline. We discuss the document and word level formulations of the language identification task, briefly discuss supervised solutions, and then present low-supervision methods based on polyglot training that are highly applicable in low-resource settings. We then discuss code mixing, a linguistic phenomenon common in bilingual and multilingual speakers. We extend our language identification methods to model code mixing and measure the extent of English-Hindi code mixing in various social media data sets.

Keywords Language identification · Supervised language identification · Unsupervised language identification · Word language identification · Polyglot document embeddings · Code mixing · Multilinguality

In Chap. 2 we motivated the value of low-resource NLP through the increasing levels of multilinguality online. We now introduce the first set of methods to model and analyze multilingual text—identifying the language a document or a word is authored in. NLP resources are more often than not monolingual. Annotators can be hard to procure for many widely used languages in an area and thus identifying a document's language can allow for the right resources to be applied to the text analysis task at hand.

The language identification problem has been extensively studied [12]—both on formal text and short-noisy social media text. Large scale language identification systems trained on milllions of examples are available [6, 7, 15, 16]. However, such systems only support slightly over a hundred languages in most cases and are inadequate to model the linguistic diversity of global social media platforms [17, 25].

Social media text presents additional challenges. Phenomena like code mixing cause multiple languages to appear within the same short text boundary. It is thus hard to precisely formulate the language identification task in many domains and estimates show that between 3–4% of documents on social media are code mixed [29]. In addition, the short, noisy nature of social media content poses difficulties even for human annotators [20].

In this chapter we cover two formulations of the problem—document-level, and word-level. The solutions for both these variants are closely related. As a further step, we introduce methods to address and model code mixing. We first explore the traditional supervised methods used to solve these problems and then introduce powerful unsupervised methods.

- **Document language identification** Given an input document (in a social media setting, this is typically a social media post or short text, like a Tweet, Facebook post, YouTube comment and so on.), we return a language label.
- **Word language identification** Given an input word, we return a language label.

4.1   Supervised Document Language Identification

Supervised settings utilize a labeled data set containing documents (words) annotated with a language label. A text classifier is then trained on this data set. A variety of design choices such as tokenization, document (word) feature representation, and the learning algorithm can impact the performance of supervised language identification systems. We discuss tokenization methods, and feature representations briefly:

Tokenization: Tokenization breaks up a document string into a sequence of distinct tokens [38]. A variety of methods are employed in NLP systems ranging from using whitespace (spaces and newline characters) as token boundaries [23], BPE [33], WordPiece [32], and SentencePiece [22]. Note that not all methods generalize across languages. For instance, Mandarin Chinese is written without spaces between characters and words [1]. Tokenizers like SentencePiece [22] are language-independent.

Feature Representation: Language identification systems construct a vector representation for an input document (word). Existing systems have incorporated character-level statistics [18, 28], and sub-word information [6, 15, 16, 26] among others. A detailed survey of various feature representations for language identification is presented in the survey by Jauhiainen et al. [12].

Given a feature representation for a document and an associated language label, we can pose the language identification problem as a classification task. A variety of large scale systems [6, 7] are trained on large data sets consisting of documents and an associated language label. Some data sets typically used for such systems include the Tatoeba corpus [36, 37], and Wikipedia [8, 39]. A broad description of various supervised systems is available in the survey by Jauhiainen et al. [12].

4.2   Supervised Word Language Identification

A straightforward method to build word-level language identification systems is to repurpose document-level systems and treat a word as an individual document.

However, such tasks are ill-posed in many settings. For instance, consider the word
to. `to` is a frequently occurring word in both English as a preposition (`I am
headed to the mall`), and in Romanized Hindi as a conjunction (`agar kam
nahin kiya to naukri jayegi`—loosely translated as *if you don't work,
then you will lose your job*). Sophisticated methods utilize information from the
word's context, such as the language label for the surrounding words [13, 34], or
model language-identification as a sequence labeling task [2, 24].

4.3   The Low Resource Setting

The supervised methods discussed above require a labeled corpus. In many settings
this is either prohibitively expensive or impossible to acquire. For instance, many
recent lines of research are aimed at social media sentiment mining of disenfranchised communities like refugees [27]. Such communities are situated in linguistically diverse areas and thus a language identification system is required before
any analysis of a corpus can be conducted. Due to circumstances like large-scale
displacement, annotators can be impossible to obtain for the desired language(s).

Another instance is that of Romanized Indic languages—where the speakers utilize the Latin alphabet instead of the traditional native script. This is particularly
pronounced in the Indian subcontinent where Romanized variants of local languages
are far more prevalent in informal settings like social media, and advertising. Large
scale corpora typically sourced from books, Wikipedia or other formal settings are
authored entirely in the native script and as a result, there exist very few (if any)
resources in the Romanized variants of these languages. NLP research on these languages has made limited progress as a result despite their extensive presence online
(see Chap. 2 for statistics).

Despite recent efforts to collect large, multilingual corpora, large scale commercial
systems are only able to support hundreds of languages [7], whereas an order of
magnitude more are needed to achieve global coverage [17].

Fortunately, recent advances in unsupervised language identification lead to very
robust solutions for low-resource settings. Solutions that require no resources beyond
the corpus itself are in fact highly desirable even for world languages like English,
especially if it manifests in noisy ways like on social media. Unsupervised solutions
take the full multilingual corpus as input and return individual monolingual subsets
as output.

Unsupervised solutions have several significant downstream applications. In cases
where no supervised solution is available, this technique eliminates the need for one.
For situations where annotation is prohibitively expensive, an annotator can label
just a few documents in a monolingual subset and those labels can be assigned to the
rest of the subset—for instance, in [25], a large scale Indic language identification
system was constructed by annotating just 200 documents and transferring labels to
millions of additional documents.

4.4 Unsupervised Language Identification

We now introduce an unsupervised language identification method designed by
Palakodety et al. [26]. The technique takes as input a multilingual corpus $\mathcal{D}$, and
produces precise and sharp monolingual components. At the root of this technique
is a key insight about the embedding spaces that result from polyglot training.

First, `FastText-100` embeddings are trained on $\mathcal{D}$. Next, for each document
$d \in \mathcal{D}$, we obtain a distinct document embedding by averaging the embeddings of
the constituent words. At this stage, we can visualize the *document embedding space*
using a t-SNE plot.

4.4.1 The Polyglot Embedding Space

Consider the t-SNE visualization of the document embeddings for a corpus $\mathcal{D}_{IndPak}$
introduced in [26] shown in Fig. 4.1. We notice three sharp distinct clusters. Manual
inspection reveals that each of the clusters is almost entirely monolingual. Furthermore, a simple clustering algorithm like k-Means can fully retrieve each of the
monolingual components.

This phenomenon has been observed across many languages and in many multilingual data sets. We show the embedding spaces resulting from one additional

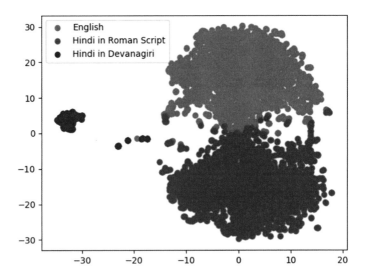

Fig. 4.1 A visualization of the polyglot document-embedding space of the corpus introduced by
Palakodety et al. [26]. Three clear clusters are visible. Inspection reveals that each cluster is a highly
precise monolingual cluster. The k-Means algorithm can be used to retrieve these components and
language labels can be assigned by inspecting just one or two documents per cluster.

Algorithm 4.1: $\mathcal{L}_{polyglot}(\mathcal{D})$

Input: $\mathcal{D}$ `// a multilingual corpus`

Output: $\mathcal{D}_k \mid k \in \{1, 2, \ldots, K\}$ `// K distinct monolingual components`

Method:
Compute `FastText-100` embeddings on $\mathcal{D}$;
Compute document embeddings $\mathcal{E}$ for each document $d \in \mathcal{D}$ by averaging constituent word embeddings;
Using *silhouettes*, pick a value K which is the number of monolingual components in $\mathcal{D}$;
Run $k-$Means with $k \leftarrow K$ on $\mathcal{E}$ yielding clusters $\mathcal{E}_k \mid k \in \{1, \ldots K\}$;
Return subsets $\mathcal{D}_k, k \in \{1, \ldots, K\}$ where $\mathcal{D}_k$ contains all the documents whose embeddings are in $\mathcal{E}_k$;

---

synthetic multilingual data set consisting of 21 European languages sourced from the original Europarl data set [21, 37] (Fig. 4.2). A full analysis across many Indo-European languages is presented by Palakodety et al. [26].

4.4.2 Retrieving Monolingual Components

Given this observation about polyglot embedding spaces, the next step involves retrieving the resulting monolingual components. A simple clustering algorithm like k-Means can successfully retrieve these components. All that remains is choosing an appropriate value for k—the number of clusters or components. Many heuristics exist for picking this hyper-parameter, and the popular *silhouettes* method [30] has been successfully applied in a variety of settings.

Once the monolingual clusters are retrieved, a language label can be assigned to each cluster by inspecting a small number (fewer than ten) of documents from each cluster. Subsequently, given a test document, a cluster assignment test can be used and the language label assigned to the chosen cluster is returned as the language label for the test document.

The full algorithm, $\mathcal{L}_{polyglot}$, is listed in Algorithm 4.1.

4.4.3 Intuition for the Method

Why does the polyglot embedding space reveal monolingual components? Recall the SkipGram objective (the basis of the `FastText-100` embeddings) - given an input word, the SkipGram model predicts its context. A Hindi word is most likely to appear in a context composed predominantly of other Hindi words. Similarly for

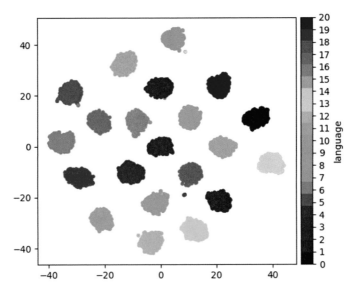

Fig. 4.2 A visualization of the polyglot document-embedding space for the Europarl data set [21, 37]. We observe 21 clusters. Inspection reveals that these are precise monolingual components. Each of the 21 monolingual subsets can be retrieved using k-Means.

English. In fact, a word's context is likely to be composed of other words authored in the same language.

The proximities among the documents captured by the resulting embeddings reflect this language-level separation—where documents written in the same language are placed closer to each other than documents authored in a different language.

4.4.4 Evaluation

We first note that the informal nature of social media data poses challenges to most state-of-the-art language identification systems. Short, noisy text is often far removed from the training data sets of these systems. Furthermore, most popular or commercial systems focus heavily on well represented world languages and thus are incapable of recognizing the low resource category that is the focus of this book. Next, given the long tail of low-resource languages, it is unlikely that every possible language is represented in the training corpus.

An unsupervised method that is solely dependent on the corpus and no other resources is thus highly useful in the low-resource setting allowing a highly diverse variety of text analyses [26, 27, 31].

Analyses show that this technique is in-fact highly competitive with commercial and large-scale supervised systems, often matching or outperforming them [26]. A detailed analysis of the method's performance on various languages in the Indo-European family, and the Indo-Aryan family show that it is a state-of-the-art technique for these language families [26].

4.4.5 Limitations

Experiments on real-world social media data sets show that languages with trace presence (less than 1% of the corpus) are often mislabeled and merged into a larger cluster [25]. This can be attributed to limitations of the k-Means algorithm and the silhouette heuristic. In general, detection of clusters in extremely skewed data sets is a difficult task and more robust clustering algorithms can be employed when necessary [14]. Further, the model depends on a whitespace tokenizer (i.e. the words in the language are separated by spacing) and is thus unsuitable for several language families without further adaptation such as using other tokenizers.

4.4.6 Downstream Applications

The technique discussed in this book has been used in a variety of real world analyses including *AI for social good* applications. For instance, unsupervised language identification was used to extract the English subset of an Indian social media corpus to analyze pro(anti)-peace sentiment in the context of the 2019 India-Pakistan crisis [26], an English subset was extracted and used to study sentiments towards the Rohingya community—a disenfranchised minority based in South Asia [27].

Unsupervised techniques are also useful in bootstrapping a large supervised solution. Considering the limitations of the unsupervised technique (arising from data set skew), an accurate, and precise *supervised* solution is desirable. An unsupervised technique can be utilized to bootstrap a large annotated data set with a significantly reduced annotation burden. We discuss one such technique introduced in [25].

Indian state boundaries were drawn along linguistic lines. Almost every state has a distinct dominant language whose Romanized variant is used extensively on social media. Most language identification systems do not have the Romanized variants of these languages as part of their training corpus. In [25], a large data set of *2.7m* social media comments authored in Romanized Indic languages from the 13 most populous Indian states is constructed using *only 260* labeled documents with the help of $\mathcal{L}_{polyglot}$.

First, a unique corpus for each of the states is constructed using comments on news videos from news networks in each state (each corpus is referred to as $\mathcal{D}_i$). Subsequently, $\mathcal{L}_{polyglot}$ is used on each $\mathcal{D}_i$ and the two largest monolingual components are retained. Retaining the largest components eliminates issues involving data set skew. The language labels assigned to each component are propagated to all cluster members and finally combined to form 1 *weakly labeled* data set.

Algorithm 4.2: $\mathcal{F}_{weakLabel}(\{\mathcal{D}_1, \ldots, \mathcal{D}_n\})$

---

foreach $\mathcal{D}_i \in \{\mathcal{D}_1, \ldots, \mathcal{D}_n\}$ **do**
    Run $\hat{\mathcal{L}}_{polyglot}$ on $\mathcal{D}_i$;
    Obtain clusters $\mathcal{C}_1, \ldots, \mathcal{C}_K$ using k-means s.t. $|\mathcal{C}_1| \geq |\mathcal{C}_2| \ldots \geq |\mathcal{C}_K|$;
    Identify $J \leq K$ dominant clusters;
    for $(j = 1; j \leq J; j = j + 1)$ **do**
        Assign language to $\mathcal{C}_j$ (denoted by $\mathcal{L}(\mathcal{C}_j)$), (supplied by the annotator);
        Sample $\gamma |\mathcal{C}_j|$ comments from $\mathcal{C}_j$ ranked by proximity from cluster center, $0 < \gamma \leq 1$;
        Add the sampled comments to $\mathcal{D}$ with *weak label* $\mathcal{L}(\mathcal{C}_j)$;

Output: Return $\mathcal{D}$

The full algorithm, $\mathcal{F}_{weakLabel}$, is shown in Algorithm 4.2. The version discussed by Palakodety et al. [25] combines an Indic data set constructed using $\mathcal{F}_{weakLabel}$ with the Tatoeba corpus [36] to produce a language identification system that is capable of supporting more than 300 languages.

4.5 Unsupervised Word Level Language Identification

In line with the supervised methods discussed before, $\mathcal{L}_{polyglot}$ can be re-purposed to perform word-level language identification. Treating each test input token as an individual document, $\mathcal{L}_{polyglot}$ can return a language label for the word itself.

4.5.1 Evaluation

This simple technique was evaluated on real world data [19] and found to be surprisingly robust yielding word-level language identification accuracies of 88.76% on Indic social media data sets [19].

As discussed earlier, word-level language identification, independent of the context, is an ill-defined problem. However, the simple solution discussed here is perfectly compatible with more advanced methods that incorporate the context [2, 13, 24, 34].

4.6 Measuring Code Mixing

Recall from Chap. 2 that a significant portion of the content from societies with a high concentration of bilinguals is code mixed. In such settings, assigning a language label to a code mixed document is ill defined. However, it is still of interest to quantify various aspects of such text. For a thorough treatment of code mixing and methods to model and address code mixing, see the survey by Sitaram et al. [35].

A variety of metrics have been proposed to model code mixing [3–5, 9–11]. We discuss a simple metric called the *Code Mixing Index* (*CMI*) introduced in [5]. The *CMI* measures the presence of a dominant language in a document.

4.6.1 Code Mixing Index

Consider a document d composed of n words $[w_1, \ldots, w_n]$ of which u words are neutral (no language label can be assigned). Assume d contains k distinct languages, $\{l_1, \ldots, l_k\}$. Let $\mathcal{L}(w_i)$ return the language of word w_i (or neutral if it is a neutral token). Let $\mathcal{N}(l_j)$ denote the total number of utterances of language l_j in the document. The code mixing index(*CMI*) is then defined as:

$$CMI(d) = \frac{\sum_{j=1}^{j=k} \mathcal{N}(l_j) - max_i(\mathcal{N}(l_i))}{n - u} \qquad (4.1)$$

where:

d	words $[w_1, \ldots, w_n]$
	languages $\{l_1, \ldots, l_k\}$
	neutral tokens u

$\mathcal{L}(w_i)$	language of word w_i
$\mathcal{N}(l_j)$	$\sum_{i=1}^{i=n} \mathbb{I}(\mathcal{L}(w_i) = l_j)$
$\mathbb{I}$	indicator function

In Eq. 4.1, the term $\sum_{j=1}^{j=k} \mathcal{N}(l_j)$ is the total number of tokens with a language label, and $max_i(\mathcal{N}(l_i))$ is the number of words written in the dominant language. We can intuit from the equation that $CMI \in [0, 1]$. Assume every word in d is a neutral token (for instance the document contains only numbers and dates), the *CMI* is then 0. Consider a common case, where a code mixed document is written in two languages (i.e. $k = 2$). The highest possible *CMI* score in this case is 0.5 when exactly half the document is written in one language and the other half in another. Thus, a low *CMI* score indicates a low level of code mixing. Conversely a high *CMI* score indicates a high level of code mixing.

We illustrate the *CMI* score further with examples of code mixed documents authored using English (colored blue), Romanized Hindi (colored red), and neutral tokens (colored black):

[**bilkul sahi baat kahi aapne imran khan** saab

please please no more war only peace][1] (loosely translates to *You've spoken the absolute truth Mr. Imran Khan, please no more war, only peace..* In this document, $\mathcal{N}(en) = 7$, $\mathcal{N}(h_e) = 6$, $n = 15$, and $u = 2$. Thus, the *CMI* is $\frac{7+6-7}{15-2}$ = 0.46.

[yeh **word** kis **language** ka hai] (loosely translates to *which language does this word belong to.*). In this document, $\mathcal{N}(en) = 2$, $\mathcal{N}(h_e) = 4$, $n = 6$, and $u = 0$. Thus, the *CMI* is $\frac{2+4-4}{6-0} = 0.33$.

[**I am the president of the company**]. In this document, $\mathcal{N}(en) = 7$, $n = 7$, and $u = 0$. Thus, the *CMI* is $\frac{7-7}{7} = 0$, indicating no code mixing.

[**main yaha rahta hoon**] (loosely translates to *I live here*). In this document, $\mathcal{N}(h_e) = 4$, $n = 4$, and $u = 0$. Thus, the *CMI* is $\frac{4-4}{4} = 0$, indicating no code mixing.

A *CMI* higher than 0.4 is a common choice of a threshold for highly code mixed documents [19].

4.6.2 The Extent of Code Mixing

We now investigate the extent of code mixing in two Indian social media data sets. We consider the corpora: (i) $\mathcal{D}_{IndPak}$: YouTube comments posted in response to Indian news videos during a period from 14th February 2019 to 13th March 2019 introduced by Palakodety et al. [26] during the 2019 India-Pakistan conflict, and (ii) $\mathcal{D}_{Covid}$: YouTube comments posted in response to India news videos during a period between 30 January, 2020 and 10 April, 2020—during the first global outbreak of COVID-19.

We use $\mathcal{L}_{polyglot}$ for the word-level language labeling trained on both corpora individually and plot the *CMI* scores for the subset of the corpus authored in Romanized Hindi or English (or both)—the most common code mixed pair in the Indian subcontinent.

We plot the percentage of the corpus within a fixed *CMI* bucket in Fig. 4.3. We observe that the bulk of both the corpora lies in the low-*CMI* range—indicating that near about 60% of the web content is almost entirely monolingual. Under 10% of the corpus is highly code-mixed. On other social media platforms like Twitter, studies report that approximately 3–4% of the corpus is code mixed [29].

---

[1] Example from Khuda Bukhsh et al. [19].

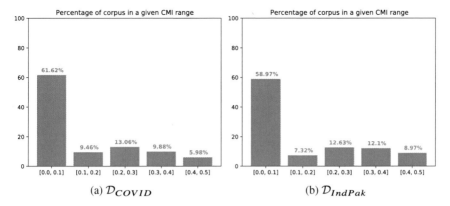

Fig. 4.3 English—Romanized Hindi code mixing statistics from two Indian social media corpora. In both data we see a similar proportion of code mixing. The bulk of the corpus (60%) exhibits very little code-mixing.

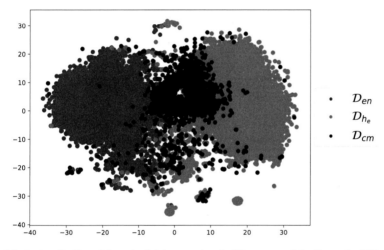

Fig. 4.4 A visualization of the polyglot document-embedding space of the Romanized Hindi and English subset of the corpus $\mathcal{D}_{IndPak}$. The two clusters corresponding to English and Hindi are visible. We notice that the Hindi-English code mixed documents lie at the boundary of both document clusters.

4.6.3 Code Mixing and the Polyglot Embedding Space

Recall the polyglot document-embedding space introduced earlier in this chapter. We noticed a clear language-based separation of documents. How do code-mixed documents fit into this embedding space? We first restrict the $\mathcal{D}_{IndPak}$ corpus to the Romanized Hindi ($\mathcal{D}_{h_e}$) and English ($\mathcal{D}_{en}$) components. We show a t-SNE plot of the document embeddings in this subset and color the high-*CMI* documents ($\mathcal{D}_{cm}$) in black (Fig. 4.4).

We observe that almost all the code-mixed documents lie at the boundary of the two monolingual clusters. This shows us that the polyglot document embedding space in fact captures the full richness of language use in a corpus in a very elegant and interpretive fashion. In other chapters, these and additional phenomena of polyglot document embeddings will be explored for other tasks.

References

1. (2000) EAC volume 25 cover and back matter. Early China 25:b1–b6. https://doi.org/10.1017/S0362502800004211
2. Barman U, Das A, Wagner J, Foster J (2014) Code mixing: a challenge for language identification in the language of social media. In: Proceedings of the first workshop on computational approaches to code switching, pp 13–23
3. Barnett R, Codó E, Eppler E, Forcadell M, Gardner-Chloros P, van Hout R, Moyer M, Torras MC, Turell MT, Sebba M, Starren M, Wensing S, (2000) The Lides coding manual: a document for preparing and analyzing language interaction data version 1.1, July 1999. Int J Bilingualism 4(2):131–132. https://doi.org/10.1177/13670069000040020101
4. Bullock B, Guzmán W, Serigos J, Sharath V, Toribio AJ (2018) Predicting the presence of a matrix language in code-switching. In: Proceedings of the third workshop on computational approaches to linguistic code-switching. Association for Computational Linguistics, Melbourne, pp 68–75. https://doi.org/10.18653/v1/W18-3208, https://aclanthology.org/W18-3208
5. Das A, Gambäck B (2014) Identifying languages at the word level in code-mixed Indian social media text. In: Proceedings of the 11th international conference on natural language processing, NLP Association of India, Goa, pp 378–387. https://www.aclweb.org/anthology/W14-5152
6. FastText (2016) Language identification. https://fasttext.cc/docs/en/language-identification.html
7. Google Cloud Translation (2021) Detecting languages. https://cloud.google.com/translate/docs/basic/detecting-language
8. Guo M, Dai Z, Vrandecic D, Al-Rfou R (2020) Wiki-40b: multilingual language model dataset. In: LREC 2020. http://www.lrec-conf.org/proceedings/lrec2020/pdf/2020.lrec-1.296.pdf
9. Guzman GA, Serigos J, Bullock BE, Toribio AJ (2016) Simple tools for exploring variation in code-switching for linguists. In: Proceedings of the second workshop on computational approaches to code switching. Association for Computational Linguistics, Austin, pp 12–20. https://doi.org/10.18653/v1/W16-5802. https://aclanthology.org/W16-5802
10. Guzmán GA, Ricard J, Serigos J, Bullock B, Toribio AJ (2017) Moving code-switching research toward more empirically grounded methods. In: CDH@ TLT, pp 1–9
11. Guzmán GA, Ricard J, Serigos J, Bullock BE, Toribio AJ (2017) Metrics for modeling code-switching across corpora. In: INTERSPEECH
12. Jauhiainen T, Lui M, Zampieri M, Baldwin T, Lindén K (2019) Automatic language identification in texts: a survey. J Artif Intell Res 65:675–782
13. Jhamtani H, Bhogi SK, Raychoudhury V (2014) Word-level language identification in bilingual code-switched texts. In: PACLIC
14. Jin X, Han J (2010) K-Medoids clustering. Springer, Boston, pp 564–565
15. Joulin A, Grave E, Bojanowski P, Douze M, Jégou H, Mikolov T (2016) Fasttext.zip: compressing text classification models. arXiv preprint arXiv:161203651
16. Joulin A, Grave E, Bojanowski P, Mikolov T (2016b) Bag of tricks for efficient text classification. arXiv preprint arXiv:160701759
17. Jurgens D, Tsvetkov Y, Jurafsky D (2017) Incorporating dialectal variability for socially equitable language identification. In: Proceedings of the 55th Annual Meeting of the Association

for Computational Linguistics, vol 2: Short Papers. Association for Computational Linguistics, Vancouver, pp 51–57. https://doi.org/10.18653/v1/P17-2009. https://aclanthology.org/P17-2009

18. Kerwin TP (2006) Classification of natural language based on character frequency
19. KhudaBukhsh AR, Palakodety S, Carbonell JG (2020) Harnessing code switching to transcend the linguistic barrier. In: Bessiere C (ed) Proceedings of the Twenty-Ninth international joint conference on artificial intelligence, IJCAI-20. International joint conferences on artificial intelligence organization, pp 4366–4374, special track on AI for CompSust and Human well-being
20. Kim S, Weber I, Wei L, Oh A (2014) Sociolinguistic analysis of twitter in multilingual societies. In: Proceedings of the 25th ACM conference on hypertext and social media. Association for Computing Machinery, New York, HT '14, pp 243–248. https://doi.org/10.1145/2631775.2631824.
21. Koehn P (2005) Europarl: a parallel corpus for statistical machine translation. MT Summit 5:79–86
22. Kudo T, Richardson J (2018) SentencePiece: a simple and language independent subword tokenizer and detokenizer for neural text processing. In: Proceedings of the 2018 conference on empirical methods in natural language processing: system demonstrations. Association for Computational Linguistics, Brussels, pp 66–71. https://doi.org/10.18653/v1/D18-2012. https://aclanthology.org/D18-2012
23. Manning CD, Raghavan P, Schütze H (2008) Introduction to information retrieval. Cambridge University Press, Cambridge. http://nlp.stanford.edu/IR-book/information-retrieval-book.html
24. Nguyen DP, Dogruoz A (2013) Word level language identification in online multilingual communication. Association for Computational Linguistics
25. Palakodety S, KhudaBukhsh A (2020) Annotation efficient language identification from weak labels. In: Proceedings of the sixth workshop on noisy user-generated text (W-NUT 2020). Association for Computational Linguistics, Online, pp 181–192. https://doi.org/10.18653/v1/2020.wnut-1.24. https://www.aclweb.org/anthology/2020.wnut-1.24
26. Palakodety S, KhudaBukhsh AR, Carbonell JG (2020a) Hope speech detection: a computational analysis of the voice of peace. In: Giacomo GD, Catalá A, Dilkina B, Milano M, Barro S, Bugarín A, Lang J (eds) ECAI 2020—24th European conference on artificial intelligence. Frontiers in artificial intelligence and applications. IOS Press, vol 325, pp 1881–1889. https://doi.org/10.3233/FAIA200305.
27. Palakodety S, KhudaBukhsh AR, Carbonell JG (2020b) Voice for the voiceless: active sampling to detect comments supporting the Rohingyas. In: Proceedings of the AAAI conference on artificial intelligence, vol 34(01), pp 454–462
28. Ranaivo-Malancon B (2006) Automatic identification of close languages—case study: Malay and Indonesian. ECTI Trans Compute Inf Technol (ECTI-CIT) 2. https://doi.org/10.37936/ecti-cit.200622.53288
29. Rijhwani S, Sequiera R, Choudhury M, Bali K, Maddila CS (2017) Estimating code-switching on Twitter with a novel generalized word-level language detection technique. In: Proceedings of the 55th Annual Meeting of the Association for Computational Linguistics, vol 1: Long Papers. Association for Computational Linguistics, Vancouver, pp 1971–1982. https://doi.org/10.18653/v1/P17-1180. https://aclanthology.org/P17-1180
30. Rousseeuw PJ (1987) Silhouettes: a graphical aid to the interpretation and validation of cluster analysis. J Comput Applied Math 20:53–65
31. Sarkar R, Mahinder S, Sarkar H, KhudaBukhsh A (2020) Social media attributions in the context of water crisis. In: Proceedings of the 2020 conference on empirical methods in natural language processing (EMNLP). Association for Computational Linguistics, Online, pp 1402–1412. DOIurl10.18653/v1/2020.emnlp-main.109. https://www.aclweb.org/anthology/2020.emnlp-main.109
32. Schuster M, Nakajima K (2012) Japanese and Korean voice search. In: 2012 IEEE international conference on acoustics, speech and signal processing (ICASSP), pp 5149–5152. https://doi.org/10.1109/ICASSP.2012.6289079

33. Sennrich R, Haddow B, Birch A (2016) Neural machine translation of rare words with subword units. In: Proceedings of the 54th annual meeting of the association for computational linguistics, vol 1: Long Papers. Association for Computational Linguistics, Berlin, pp 1715–1725. https://doi.org/10.18653/v1/P16-1162. https://aclanthology.org/P16-1162
34. Shirvani R, Piergallini M, Gautam GS, Chouikha M (2016) The Howard University system submission for the shared task in language identification in Spanish-English codeswitching. In: Proceedings of the second workshop on computational approaches to code switching. Association for Computational Linguistics, Austin, pp 116–120. https://doi.org/10.18653/v1/W16-5815. https://aclanthology.org/W16-5815
35. Sitaram S, Chandu KR, Rallabandi SK, Black AW (2019) A survey of code-switched speech and language processing. arXiv preprint arXiv:190400784
36. Tatoeba (2021) Tatoeba. https://tatoeba.org/eng/downloads, online. Accessed 01 July 2021
37. Tiedemann J (2012) Parallel data, tools and interfaces in OPUS. In: Proceedings of the Eighth international conference on language resources and evaluation (LREC'12). European Language Resources Association (ELRA), Istanbul
38. Webster JJ, Kit C (1992) Tokenization as the initial phase in NLP. In: Proceedings of the 14th conference on computational linguistics, vol 4. Association for Computational Linguistics, USA, COLING '92, pp 1106–1110. https://doi.org/10.3115/992424.992434.
39. Wikimedia Foundation (2021) Wikimedia downloads. https://dumps.wikimedia.org, online. Accessed 3 June 2020

Chapter 5
Low Resource Machine Translation

Abstract We discuss the burgeoning field of unsupervised machine translation, where words and phrases are translated between languages without any parallel corpora. We discuss popular methods, and applications to low-resource settings. We further investigate the application of polyglot training to this field and present new promising directions for unsupervised machine translation.

Keywords Machine translation · Word by word translation · Unsupervised machine translation · Polyglot document embedding

Machine translation is one of the most promising lines of research for low-resource NLP. Access to perfect machine translation essentially eliminates any resource constraints across languages as corpora authored and annotated in a world language can be trivially translated to the low-resource language or setting.

On well-resourced language pairs (English and German for instance), machine translation methods have achieved exceptional success [4, 16, 17]. However, a significant number of language pairs are poorly supported by modern machine translation systems. In this chapter, we will discuss some machine translation methods that are incredibly resource efficient. We begin by briefly discussing supervised methods for well-resourced languages. We then discuss the low-resource setting and how modern methods overcome the resource constraints.

5.1 The Supervised Problem

Supervised machine translation methods operate on a parallel corpus containing sentences in a source language and their corresponding translations in a target language. Neural machine translation methods have achieved better than human performance on several language-pairs [4, 15–17]. A variety of architectures have been proposed in recent years [15] and active research continues to construct larger-scale corpora for more language pairs [20, 21].

5.2 The Low-Resource Setting

Solutions for low-resource machine translation depend mostly on the extent of resources available. Modern methods are able to operate solely on monolingual corpora [3], incorporate bilingual lexicon or similar resources when they are available [12], and in some cases even uncover relationships across languages even when no monolingual corpora are available [8].

We cover three solutions generally applicable in low-resource settings. The first solution utilizes monolingual corpora and a dictionary between the source and target languages to build a word-translation system. We then discuss methods that eliminate the need for a dictionary and directly construct word translation systems from monolingual corpora and explore methods that deal with the even more extreme case that eliminate the need for monolingual corpora.

5.3 Word Translation with Small Bilingual Data

In this setting, we have access to monolingual corpora in the source and target languages, and a small dictionary (on the order of a few thousand words) between these languages. Mikolov et al. [12] provide a simple solution for this setting. As a first step, SkipGram word embeddings are trained on the monolingual corpora yielding two sets of embeddings—say $\mathcal{E}_s$ and $\mathcal{E}_t$ for the source and target languages respectively. The dictionary is composed of word pairs $\langle s_i, t_i \rangle$ in the provided dictionary. Word translation is essentially a linear transformation, W, mapping points in $\mathcal{E}_s$ to points in $\mathcal{E}_t$. This is achieved by solving the optimization problem in Eq. 5.1.

$$\min_W \sum_i \| W s_i - t_i \|^2 \tag{5.1}$$

This can be trained using stochastic gradient descent and a suitable W matrix is obtained. Given a test word s in the source language, we first obtain its embedding e_s, transform it to the embedding space of the target language by computing $W e_s$ and then retrieving the word t whose embedding e_t is closest to $W e_s$.

This simple method is surprisingly effective on a variety of language pairs including pairs from distant language families like English-Vietnamese.

5.4 Word Translation with *Smaller* Bilingual Data

The technique discussed above uses a dictionary of a few thousand word-pairs. In many low-resource settings this can be prohibitively expensive or even impossible to obtain. A simple extension by Artetxe et al. [2] reduces this requirement to a dictionary of only a few dozen word pairs, in some cases as few as 25. The technique follows an iterative procedure—constructing a transformation from the source embedding space to the target, growing the dictionary using this transformation, and using this new dictionary to learn a newer and more improved transformation. The process is repeated until a convergence criterion is reached.

Formally, we are given embeddings $\mathcal{E}_s$ and $\mathcal{E}_t$ for the source and target languages respectively. A weight matrix W is learned during the process. A matrix D encodes the dictionary and D_{ij} is set to 1 if the ith source word is related to the jth target word. At each iteration, we improve W^* using:

$$W^* = \min_W \sum_i \sum_j D_{ij} \left\| \mathcal{E}_{s_i} W - \mathcal{E}_{t_j} \right\|^2 \tag{5.2}$$

In Eq. 5.2 we find a transform matrix W that can transform a dictionary entry's source word embedding $\mathcal{E}_{s_i}$ to its target word embedding $\mathcal{E}_{t_j}$.

At each iteration, D is also updated by setting D_{ij} to 1, if the jth target word's embedding, $\mathcal{E}_{t_j}$, is closest to the ith source word's embedding when transformed with W. This is accomplished with a simple dot-product test:

$$D_{ij} = 1, \text{ if } j = arg\,max_k \mathcal{E}_{s_i} W \cdot \mathcal{E}_{t_k} \tag{5.3}$$

A dictionary on the order of a few dozen word pairs is fairly straightforward to construct even in low-resource settings. Artetxe et al. recommend numerals as a seed dictionary. Arabic numerals are common across most online communities even where the Latin alphabet is uncommon [1, 22] and thus can serve as a seed dictionary between very distant language pairs. In many cases, loan words, numbers and dates of events can serve as a seed dictionary as well [8].

The convergence criterion used to terminate the iterative process is based on Eq. 5.3—if the average dot-product drops below a threshold, we terminate the iteration process.

5.5 Unsupervised Word Translation

The solutions thus far all utilize a seed dictionary that is used as-is or progressively grown during training. Recent solutions show that this requirement can be fully relaxed and a word translation system can be built solely using monolingual corpora [3]. Conneau et al. also propose learning a transformation matrix W and use an adversarial learning process [7] where a discriminator network learns to distinguish a transformed source embedding (using W) from a target embedding. W is trained to confuse this discriminator network.

5.6 Polyglot Training for Unsupervised Machine Translation

Thus far, we have seen that polyglot training, where a single model (in this case `FastText-100` embeddings) is trained on a multilingual corpus, reveals monolingual clusters (Chap. 4), and provides a geometric interpretation for code mixing (Chap. 4). Recent results show that the polyglot training scheme also reveals bilingual lexicons or dictionaries [8]. This phenomenon was discovered using a selective nearest-neighbor sampling in the polyglot word-embedding space. Consider a source word s authored in language $\mathcal{L}_1$ that we intend to translate to language $\mathcal{L}_2$. In addition, we denote $\mathcal{W}_{\mathcal{L}_1}$ as the set of all words authored in $\mathcal{L}_1$, and $\mathcal{W}_{\mathcal{L}_2}$ as the set of all words authored in $\mathcal{L}_2$ respectively. Note that $\mathcal{W}_{\mathcal{L}_1}$ and $\mathcal{W}_{\mathcal{L}_2}$ can be trivially retrieved using the unsupervised $\mathcal{L}_{polyglot}$ algorithm discussed in Algorithm 4.1. The target translation of s, t is obtained in this scheme by finding the nearest neighbor to the embedding of s restricted to the set $\mathcal{W}_{\mathcal{L}_2}$. This surprisingly simple nearest-neighbor sampling method can retrieve substantial bilingual lexicon across various language pairs including English-Romanized Hindi.

Figure 5.1 illustrates the sampling scheme.

Ablation studies reveal that this phenomenon is caused due to a variety of factors—first, in Indic social media, a significant portion of the corpus is code mixed with a high degree of lexical borrowing, and a high frequency of loan words from English to Romanized Hindi. Numbers, and dates are consistent across both the languages given that Romanized Hindi uses Arabic numerals.

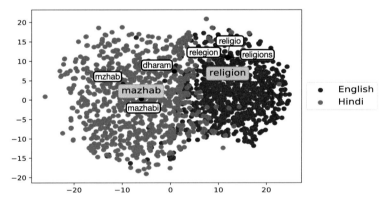

Fig. 5.1 A t-SNE 2D visualization of Skip-gram polyglot embeddings trained on (a) a data set of 2.04 million YouTube comments relevant to the 2019 India-Pakistan conflict [13]. Three nearest neighbors (using cosine distance) of the Hindi word *mazhab* "religion" and the English word *religion* are highlighted. These results indicate that naive nearest neighbor sampling of a word yields other words with similar meaning in the same language. Selective nearest neighbor sampling only in the target language subset however reveals the correct word translation

5.7 Phrase Translation

Thus far, we have discussed methods to implement word translation. A few solutions exist to build phrase or sentence level translation. Lample et al. [9] propose a multi-stage pipeline that operates directly on monolingual corpora. First, a word translation system is constructed using one of the methods discussed previously. A three phase process is subsequently used for translating sentences. As an initial pass, given a sentence as input, a *word-by-word translation* is obtained. Next, a language model in the target language is used to perform local substitutions and re-orderings—i.e. *denoising*. A denoising autoencoder is used for this stage [18]. Finally, a *back-translation* step [14]. In *back-translation*, a target language sentence (from the target language monolingual corpus) is translated back to the source language and this *back-translated* sentence and target language sentence are used as supervision in an iterative fashion. Essentially, the last step is a noisy, supervised phrase-translation step where the supervised sentence pair consists of an actual target language sentence (the target) and a noisy *back-translated* source sentence (the source).

Back-translation is a powerful technique that has been applied even to improve word translation systems [8] and also for large-scale supervised machine translation systems [4].

5.8 Limitations

A variety of factors influence the performance of word translation systems. Despite their success, recent evidence [19] calls into question the stability of these methods [11]. On very poorly resourced language pairs from distant language families (Nepali-English, Sinhalese-English), unsupervised methods are shown to perform rather poorly [6]. In addition, domain-mismatch between the monolingual corpora can cause the unsupervised method to perform rather poorly even in well-resourced settings.

Evidence suggests multilinguality is key to improving unsupervised machine translation on distant and poorly-resourced language families [5, 10]. Instead of training a dictionary solely between the language pair in question, a larger model to and from multiple languages is trained. Intending to translate to and from English, Garcia et al. [5] use Turkish, Gujarati, Kazakh, Nepali, (the poorly resourced set), and Russian, Hindi, Telugu, Tamil, and Chinese (the better resourced set). Russian is included for similarity to Kazakh, the Indic languages Telugu, Hindi, and Tamil are included for similarity to Gujarati, Nepali, and Sinhalese and finally Chinese for the size of the monolingual corpus. The resulting models outperform even existing supervised baselines in many cases.

References

1. Alsulami A (2019) A sociolinguistic analysis of the use of Arabizi in social media among Saudi Arabians. Int J Engl Linguis 9:257. https://doi.org/10.5539/ijel.v9n6p257
2. Artetxe M, Labaka G, Agirre E (2017) Learning bilingual word embeddings with (almost) no bilingual data. In: ACL
3. Conneau A, Lample G, Ranzato M, Denoyer L, Jégou H (2017) Word translation without parallel data. arXiv preprint arXiv:171004087
4. Edunov S, Ott M, Auli M, Grangier D (2018) Understanding back-translation at scale. In: Proceedings of the 2018 conference on empirical methods in natural language processing, Association for Computational Linguistics, Brussels, pp 489–500. https://doi.org/10.18653/v1/D18-1045. https://aclanthology.org/D18-1045
5. Garcia X, Siddhant A, Firat O, Parikh A (2021) Harnessing multilinguality in unsupervised machine translation for rare languages. In: Proceedings of the 2021 conference of the North American Chapter of the Association for Computational Linguistics: Human Language Technologies. Association for Computational Linguistics, Online, pp 1126–1137. https://doi.org/10.18653/v1/2021.naacl-main.89. https://aclanthology.org/2021.naacl-main.89
6. Guzmán F, Chen PJ, Ott M, Pino J, Lample G, Koehn P, Chaudhary V, Ranzato M (2019) The FLORES evaluation datasets for low-resource machine translation: Nepali–English and Sinhala–English. In: Proceedings of the 2019 conference on Empirical methods in natural language processing and the 9th international joint conference on natural language processing (EMNLP-IJCNLP), Association for Computational Linguistics, Hong Kong, China, pp 6098–6111. https://doi.org/10.18653/v1/D19-1632. https://aclanthology.org/D19-1632
7. Karras T, Aittala M, Hellsten J, Laine S, Lehtinen J, Aila T (2020) Training generative adversarial networks with limited data. In: Larochelle H, Ranzato M, Hadsell R, Balcan MF, Lin H (eds) Advances in neural information processing systems. Curran Associates, Inc., vol 33, pp 12104–12114. https://proceedings.neurips.cc/paper/2020/file/8d30aa96e72440759f74bd2306c1fa3d-Paper.pdf
8. KhudaBukhsh AR, Palakodety S, Mitchell TM (2020) Discovering bilingual lexicons in polyglot word embeddings. CoRR abs/2008.13347, https://arxiv.org/abs/2008.13347, 2008.13347
9. Lample G, Ott M, Conneau A, Denoyer L, Ranzato M (2018) Phrase-based & neural unsupervised machine translation. In: Proceedings of the 2018 conference on empirical methods in natural language processing. Association for Computational Linguistics, Brussels, pp 5039–5049. https://doi.org/10.18653/v1/D18-1549. https://aclanthology.org/D18-1549
10. Liu Y, Gu J, Goyal N, Li X, Edunov S, Ghazvininejad M, Lewis M, Zettlemoyer L (2020) Multilingual denoising pre-training for neural machine translation. Trans Associ Comput Linguist 8:726–742
11. Marchisio K, Duh K, Koehn P (2020) When does unsupervised machine translation work? In: Proceedings of the fifth conference on machine translation. Association for Computational Linguistics, Online, pp 571–583. https://aclanthology.org/2020.wmt-1.68
12. Mikolov T, Le QV, Sutskever I (2013) Exploiting similarities among languages for machine translation. ArXiv abs/1309.4168
13. Palakodety S, KhudaBukhsh AR, Carbonell JG (2020) Hope speech detection: a computational analysis of the voice of peace. In: Giacomo GD, Catalá A, Dilkina B, Milano M, Barro S, Bugarín A, Lang J (eds) ECAI 2020—24th European conference on artificial intelligence. Frontiers in artificial intelligence and applications. IOS Press, vol 325, pp 1881–1889. https://doi.org/10.3233/FAIA200305. https://doi.org/10.3233/FAIA200305
14. Sennrich R, Haddow B, Birch A (2016) Improving neural machine translation models with monolingual data. In: Proceedings of the 54th Annual Meeting of the Association for Computational Linguistics (Volume 1: Long Papers), Association for Computational Linguistics, Berlin, pp 86–96. https://doi.org/10.18653/v1/P16-1009. https://aclanthology.org/P16-1009
15. Stahlberg F (2019) Neural machine translation: a review and survey. arXiv: Computation and Language

16. Takase S, Kiyono S (2021a) Lessons on parameter sharing across layers in transformers. ArXiv abs/2104.06022
17. Takase S, Kiyono S (2021b) Rethinking perturbations in encoder-decoders for fast training. In: Proceedings of the 2021 conference of the North American Chapter of the Association for Computational Linguistics: Human Language Technologies. Association for Computational Linguistics, Online, pp 5767–5780. https://doi.org/10.18653/v1/2021.naacl-main.460. https://aclanthology.org/2021.naacl-main.460
18. Vincent P, Larochelle H, Bengio Y, Manzagol PA (2008) Extracting and composing robust features with denoising autoencoders. In: Proceedings of the 25th international conference on Machine learning, pp 1096–1103
19. Vulić I, Glavaš G, Reichart R, Korhonen A (2019) Do we really need fully unsupervised cross-lingual embeddings? In: Proceedings of the 2019 conference on empirical methods in natural language processing and the 9th international joint conference on natural language processing (EMNLP-IJCNLP). Association for Computational Linguistics, Hong Kong, pp 4407–4418. https://doi.org/10.18653/v1/D19-1449. https://aclanthology.org/D19-1449
20. WMT20 (2021) Fifth conference on machine translation (wmt20). https://www.statmt.org/wmt20/
21. WMT21 (2021) Sixth conference on machine translation (wmt21). https://www.statmt.org/wmt21/
22. Zhang Y (2017) The semiotic multifunctionality of Arabic numerals in Chinese online discourse. Language@Internet 14

Chapter 6
Semantic Sampling

Abstract A variety of tasks involving social media text require mining rare samples. In text classification, information retrieval, and other NLP tasks, working with very skewed or imbalanced data sets poses many challenges. In such settings, training data sets can be rapidly bootstrapped using highly targeted sampling strategies. This chapter draws on work in active learning, semantic similarity, and sampling strategies to address a variety of social media text mining tasks. The topics involved are particularly well suited for social media analysis. Most tasks surrounding user generated social media text such as content moderation, and recommendations often involve rapid model construction in response to real world events in real time. The methods discussed allow task-specific data sets and models to be constructed rapidly often using just a handful of initial samples. We then explore extensions to sample across languages—allowing powerful pipelines that can transfer resources from well-resourced languages to their low-resource counterparts.

Keywords Active learning · Cross lingual sampling · Semantic sampling · Rare positive mining · Certainty sampling · Uncertainty sampling

Content moderation and content discovery are among the most important tasks in mining social media text data. Filtering out the desired data from a social media corpus is often modeled as a text classification problem. A labeled, balanced data set of positive and negative examples (in the binary case) is therefore a pre-requisite to build robust systems. Due to the immense amount of user generated content on large social media platforms, constructing this training data set involves mining and discovering a rare subset of the full corpus. We discuss a few examples of such tasks:

Hate speech **detection**: *hate speech* detection is an important focus area for many important social media platforms like Facebook, and Twitter. While different platforms use different definitions of *hate speech* [1, 14, 31], a general consistent definition is that *hate speech* is speech that targets certain potentially disadvantaged social groups in ways that might be harmful to them [12, 15]. Estimates show that on Twitter, hate speech is less than 1% of the total number of posts at any given time [26]. Statistics revealed by Facebook show that around 10 out of every 10,000 posts viewed on Facebook are hate speech [9] (i.e. around 0.1%).

S. Palakodety et al., *Low Resource Social Media Text Mining*, SpringerBriefs in Computer Science, https://doi.org/10.1007/978-981-16-5625-5_6
49

***Help speech* detection**: Palakodety et al. defined *help speech* [25] as content championing the cause of disenfranchised communities in the context of the Rohingya refugee crisis [32]. Inspection of a random sample of the corpus showed that only 10.67% of the content was *help speech*.

***Hope speech* detection**: Palakodety et al. defined *hope speech* [24] as hostility diffusing content in the context of the 2019 India-Pakistan conflict [4]. Inspection of a random sample of the English subset revealed that only 2.45% of the content was *hope speech*. A later analysis [17] revealed that only 1.8% of the Romanized Hindi subset was *hope speech*.

***Fear speech* detection**: Introduced by Buyse [5], *fear speech* is defined as "an expression aimed at instilling (existential) fear of a target (ethnic or religious) group". Out of a corpus of 2.7m posts in public Indian political WhatsApp groups (only a tiny fraction of all WhatsApp groups), a small fraction of posts were considered as *fear speech* [27].

Birth defect post detection: In an analysis done by Klein et al. [20], from a random sample of pregnancy-related tweets, fewer than 5% of the tweets mentioned birth defects and fewer than 10% of tweets were deemed "possible defect" by annotators. Note that the base corpus underwent significant filtering and the proportions in regards to the full twitter feed are going to be minuscule.

Across all these tasks, we discover that building supervised data sets for classification or other tasks involves handling *rare positives*—i.e. the class distribution is skewed and the *positive* class is exceedingly rare in the corpus but enough of these have to be obtained from the corpus to train a classifier.

In low-resource text mining tasks, the effects are even more pronounced. As discussed in Chap. 2, annotation is difficult or impossible in many low-resource tasks. In this chapter, we discuss tools and social media analysis case-studies to mine these rare positives.

We first begin by discussing Active Learning—a branch of machine learning concerned with progressively improving weak classifiers by growing and curating the data set they are trained on. Then we discuss a few case studies on real world social media data sets.

6.1 Active Learning

In active learning, using a classifier C trained on a data set D, and an unlabeled pool of examples U, we progressively improve C by selecting examples from U, annotating these and then add these new examples to the data set D, yielding D'. The classifier C is then retrained on this newer data set, D', to yield a new classifier with improved performance.

Exactly which examples are chosen from U is determined by which aspects of the classifier C need improving. For instance, we might choose to improve the precision of C, in other cases, we might choose to improve the performance on a subcategory of positive labeled examples. We next discuss some common sampling strategies and their strengths and shortcomings. For a comprehensive discussion of active learning, see the survey by Settles [29].

6.1.1 Active Learning Strategies

We start with the same setting as before: we have a classifier, C trained on data set $\mathcal{D}$ and we have access to an unlabeled pool of samples $\mathcal{U}$. Evaluating a test example using C yields a predicted label and a prediction probability.

Random Sampling: As the name suggests, we draw a random sample from $\mathcal{U}$. The resulting sample is representative of $\mathcal{U}$.

Uncertainty Sampling: In this regimen, we draw samples from $\mathcal{U}$ that C is *least confident* of [22]. A variety of metrics are available to estimate confidence. A simple method involves using the entropy of the distribution of predicted labels [11]. A variety of other methods have been proposed in recent years [10, 19, 28].

In cases where the label distribution is highly skewed or imbalanced, uncertainty sampling might perform poorly [6, 13] and stratified sampling has been proposed as an alternative.

Stratified Sampling: Stratified sampling [3] divides the unlabeled pool into homogeneous groups and then samples from these. In cases of class imbalance, this allows the minority label examples to be grouped together and discovered during the sampling phase.

Certainty Sampling: In many text mining tasks, in addition to improving recall, a major focus is improving precision. In short text settings which are typical of social media content, certainty sampling is shown to improve the precision of text classification systems [2, 16, 25, 30]. The sampling strategy prioritizes examples that the classifier is *highly confident* about.

These strategies are only a few of the wide range of methods proposed in recent years [29]. Many tasks on real world social media data sets often combine multiple strategies in one pipeline. A range of methods that combine active learning and analyses based on word or document embeddings and newer methods are widespread. For instance, Palakodety et al. utilize document embeddings as part of their active learning pipeline [25] and construct a diverse data set for a binary classification task. We next discuss a few case studies that illustrate complex pipelines for real world social media text mining tasks.

6.2 Case Studies

We now discuss a few case studies where active learning strategies are combined to mine rare positive and build robust classifiers. We emphasize that real world active learning pipelines often combine more than one strategy to improve classifiers and construct data sets. The examples discussed below all feature extreme class imbalance and skew.

6.2.1 Help Speech *Detection*

Palakodety et al. introduced the task of mining *help speech* in the context of the Rohingya refugee crisis [25]. *Help speech* includes YouTube comments supportive of a disenfranchised minority (the Rohingya refugees) in a corpus primarily full of ambivalent or negative comments. A random sampling reveals that 10.67% of comments were *help speech*. To build a classifier that detects *help speech*, a balanced data set of nearly equal positive and negative examples was constructed.

The pipeline starts with a seed set of positive and negative comments (some of which are not present in the corpus but authored by the annotators). A round of random sampling is then used to expand the corpus. *Active sampling*—nearest neighbor sampling in the `sent2vec` [23] document-embedding space is used to expand this corpus further. A round of certainty and uncertainty sampling yield a corpus of 1391 positives and 1399 negatives—i.e. nearly balanced. Note that random sampling alone yields a mere 10.67% positives. The pipeline thus allowed the construction of a data set of a few thousand documents, with a balanced number of positives and negatives, starting from approximately ten example documents.

Semantic sampling using the `sent2vec` document embeddings allows rapid construction of a balanced data set for a skewed class problem. Inspection of resulting data set reveals a diverse set of examples spanning the full range of the *help speech* definition.

A final classifier is built using n-gram features and the `sent2vec` embeddings themselves and deployed on the unlabeled, unseen corpus. An example of a comment detected by the final *help speech* classifier is shown in Table 6.1.

We notice that `sent2vec` is able to detect comments exhibiting extreme disfluency—a phenomenon commonplace in many refugee related corpora (see Chap. 2). The sub-word extensions within `sent2vec` allow it to obtain robust representations for documents with a very high degree of spelling disfluencies.

The full training pipeline is illustrated in Fig. 6.1.

Table 6.1 Selected comment detected by the *help speech* classifier introduced by Palakodety et al. [25].

thank you so for news today and vi want full human rights in arakan myanmar and stop nvc card and ples vi want myanmar army goverment to the icc kireminal courd justice and vi want full setizenthip in arakan myanmar vi no bangali vi setizenthip in arakan myanmar and myanmar army reped womens rohingya and etnik kilingsing of rohingya and genocide of rohingya and ples vi want hlep from un konsiel and from human rights wohc ples hlep stop genocide of rohingya and humanty in myanmar and thank you so lot god bles you all

The comment combines all the low-resource attributes covered in Chap. 2 including spelling and grammar disfluencies on account of English not being the author's primary language. Comment chosen solely for illustrative purposes—no opinion on the refugee crisis is intended

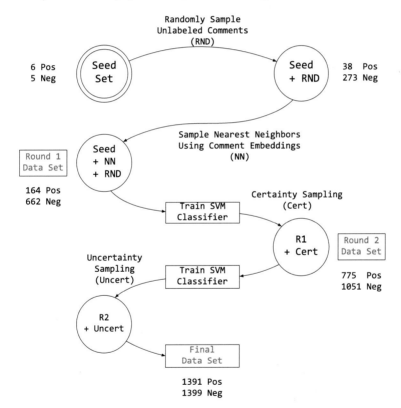

Fig. 6.1 A data set bootstrapping pipeline introduced by Palakodety et al. [25] to build a classifier to detect *help speech*.

6.2.2 Hope Speech *Detection*

Introduced by Palakodety et al. [24], *hope speech* content diffuses hostility and champions peace in the context of the 2019 India-Pakistan conflict [4]. Similar to the pipeline discussed in Sect. 6.2.1, an active learning pipeline comprising random sampling, certainty sampling, and uncertainty sampling is employed. The final data set consists of 2,277 positives and 7716 negatives. Note that this data set is an extreme case of *rare positive* mining since the base proportions of positives in the data set was approximately 1.8%.

6.3 Cross-Lingual Sampling

We now discuss the cross-lingual version of the sampling problem. Consider a multilingual corpus composed of documents authored in languages $\mathcal{L}_{1...k}$. The cross lingual sampling task takes as input a document authored in language $\mathcal{L}_i$ and returns semantically similar documents authored in $\mathcal{L}_j$ ($j \neq i$).

In the well-resourced regime, translation systems that translate between $\mathcal{L}_i$ and $\mathcal{L}_j$ can be effectively employed. We simply translate the document (and any associated annotations) from $\mathcal{L}_i$ to $\mathcal{L}_j$ and then utilize any of the semantic sampling schemes discussed in Sect. 6.1 to retrieve the desired documents.

In the low-resource setting, where one can't assume the existence of large-scale translation resources, a variety of solutions have been developed. We present three solutions here. The first utilizes one of the bilingual lexicon induction or word translation schemes introduced in Chap. 5. The polyglot training scheme is employed next to build similar systems with even fewer requirements. Finally, we explore how code mixing, often considered an impediment in NLP tasks and pipelines, can be utilized for cross-lingual sampling.

6.3.1 *Sampling With Unsupervised Machine Translation*

Cross-lingual sampling is a standard baseline task in many unsupervised translation systems [7, 8, 21]. The sampling task is typically limited to finding one document—the correct translation for an input sentence (as specified in the ground truth corpus). Depending on the translation system being tested, a translated phrase or embedding is obtained and a document that is the nearest neighbor of this translated phrase or embedding is returned.

In real world tasks, we typically want to sample a diverse collection of documents, instead of merely one. In the framework above, we can simply sample the top k nearest neighbors instead of just one and return that as the sample. An example pipeline using a word translation system is shown in Fig. 6.2. The system begins with a set of source

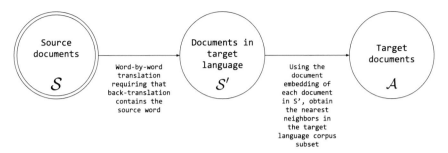

Fig. 6.2 A sample pipeline illustrating a document sampling step using a word translation system. Starting from a set of documents S, a noisy word-by-word translation S' is obtained and finally a round of nearest neighbor sampling yields A.

documents S, performs a noisy word-by-word translation of each document to obtain a set of translated documents S'. Finally, a round of nearest neighbor sampling is utilized where the nearest neighbors of each document in S' are obtained yielding documents A.

6.3.2 Sampling Using The Polyglot Embedding Space

In this book so far, we discovered that polyglot document embeddings organize a multilingual corpus into precise monolingual corpora (Sect. 4.4), provide an elegant interpretation for code mixing (Sect. 4.6.1), and even surface a substantial dictionary allowing us to build word translation systems (Sect. 5.6). These can even be adapted for the sampling task [18]. The solution proposed by KhudaBukhsh et al. [18] starts with a source document S_{source} in the source language, and constructs an embedding in the target language by sampling in the polyglot document embedding space using translateEmbedding method in Algorithm 6.1. Once a translated embedding is obtained, nearest neighbor sampling can be used to retrieve target language documents.

6.3.3 Using Code Mixing For Cross-Lingual Sampling

We introduced code mixing in Sect. 4.6.1 and measured the extent of code mixing in various real world social media data sets in Sect. 4.6.2. We now utilize code switching to perform cross lingual sampling using a technique introduced by KhudaBukhsh et al. [17].

   Consider the code mixed document[1] and its loose translation (italicized)

---

[1] Example from Khuda Bukhsh et al. [17].

Algorithm 6.1: `translateEmbedding`($\mathcal{S}_{source}$)

Input: A document $\mathcal{S}_{source}$ denoted by $[w_1,...,w_k]$
Output: A document embedding of $\mathcal{S}_{source}$ translated into $\mathcal{L}_{target}$
Dependency: *topTranslations*(w_i, N) returns N nearest neighbors of w_i from the target language vocabulary using the word translation method from KhudaBukhsh et al. [18];
Dependency: *embedding*(w_i) returns the polyglot `FastText-100` embedding of word w_i;
Initialization: $\mathcal{E} \leftarrow \{\}$
Main loop:
foreach word $w_i \in \mathcal{S}_{source}$ **do**
    if $\mathcal{L}(w_i) = \mathcal{L}_{target}$ **then**
       $\mathcal{E} \leftarrow \mathcal{E} \cup \{embedding(w_i)\}$
    else
       $\mathcal{T} \leftarrow topTranslations(w_i, N)$
       $\mathcal{C} \leftarrow \{\}$
       foreach word $w_t \in \mathcal{T}$ **do**
          if $w_i \in topTranslations(w_t, N)$ **then**
             $\mathcal{C} \leftarrow \mathcal{C} \cup \{w_t\}$
          end
       end
       if $\mathcal{C} \neq \{\}$ **then**
          randomly select w from $\mathcal{C}$
          $\mathcal{E} \leftarrow \mathcal{E} \cup \{embedding(w)\}$
       end
    end
end
Output: Average of $\mathcal{E}$

I love **India** I am **Pakistani** mein amun chahta hon khuda ke waste jang nai

peace peace peace

I love India, I am Pakistani. I want peace for God's sake, not war, peace peace peace.

In this document, say $\mathcal{L}_1$ is English (blue), $\mathcal{L}_2$ is Romanized Hindi (red), and the words India, and Pakistani are neutral tokens. We observe:

- the portions authored in $\mathcal{L}_1$ and $\mathcal{L}_2$ are semantically consistent,
- when these portions are isolated, we get two documents authored in $\mathcal{L}_1$ and $\mathcal{L}_2$ respectively, and
- the isolated portions serve as weak translations of one another

Thus, code mixed documents serve as a *bridge* between the languages used in the document. We can identify highly code mixed documents using the techniques discussed in Sect. 4.6.1. Given a corpus $\mathcal{D}$, let $\mathcal{D}_{cm}$ denote the highly code mixed sub-corpus. Once $\mathcal{D}_{cm}$ is identified, given an input document d authored in $\mathcal{L}_1$, we perform the following steps:

- Isolate the $\mathcal{L}_1$ portions of all the documents in $\mathcal{D}_{cm}$
- perform nearest neighbor sampling using only these portions and retrieve those documents in $\mathcal{D}_{cm}$ that are similar to d
- Now consider the $\mathcal{L}_2$ portions of these retrieved documents. These are document fragments similar to d but only authored in $\mathcal{L}_2$. We can retrieve the nearest neighbors of these document fragments and restrict the sampling to documents solely authored in $\mathcal{L}_2$.

Thus, we used a code mixed document as a translation step or a *bridge*. The source language portion of the code mixed document is used to match against the source language document and the corresponding target language portion is treated as the translation and used for further nearest neighbor sampling.

Figure 6.3 illustrates the polyglot embedding space. Note that the code mixed documents lie at the interface of the monolingual clusters. During our sampling, we start with the input document present in the English region. The first round of nearest neighbor sampling moves us into the code mixed region, and the next round of nearest neighbor sampling moves us to the Romanized Hindi region.

In an alternate task, a similar pipeline was used by Khudabukhsh et al. to sample comments encouraging covid guideline compliance.

KhudaBukhsh et al. [17] applied the code mixing based cross-lingual sampling method to detect *hope speech* in Romanized Hindi using a *hope speech* classifier in English. Figure 6.3 shows the polyglot document embedding space. First, the *hope speech* classifier was used to retrieve code mixed *hope speech* by predicting on the English fragments of the code mixed documents. After a round of nearest neighbor sampling, the Romanized Hindi fragments were utilized as noisy translations of the English fragments and used for further nearest neighbor sampling. The document embedding space visualization in Fig. 6.3 shows us that the final set of documents are from the Romanized Hindi region, and span a large space indicating wide topical diversity.

The sampling strategy that uses code mixing is summarized in a pipeline diagram in Fig. 6.4.

Note that in Sect. 2.3, we discussed that Hindi is often the preferred medium to express negative sentiment for Hindi-English bilinguals. KhudaBukhsh et al. reported that random sampling in the Romanized Hindi subset yields 1.8% *hope speech*. In contrast, code mixing based sampling provided a ten fold improvement.

This underscores our argument that in low-resource environments it is beneficial to transfer resources from a world language like English to a low-resource language when possible. In the above example, an existing English *hope speech* classifier was re-purposed to sample Romanized Hindi comments in the wild. The entire cross-lingual pipeline can be trained in a purely corpus dependent fashion with no external resources.

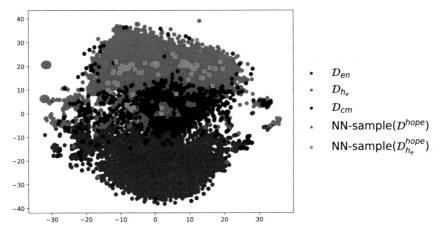

Fig. 6.3 The polyglot document embedding space showing documents retrieved from the Romanized Hindi region $\mathcal{D}_{h_e}$ using only an English ($\mathcal{D}_{en}$) classifier. Predictions are made using this classifier in the highly code mixed region $\mathcal{D}_{cm}$, a round of nearest neighbor sampling is used to expand this set (NN-sample($\mathcal{D}^{hope}$)) and then the Romanized Hindi fragments are used to sample from the exclusively monolingual Romanized Hindi subset thus performing the cross-lingual sampling

Fig. 6.4 The sampling strategy pipeline using code mixed documents to bridge English $\mathcal{D}_{en}$ and Romanized Hindi $\mathcal{D}_{h_e}$ and sample *hope speech* in Romanized Hindi using only an English *hope speech* classifier.

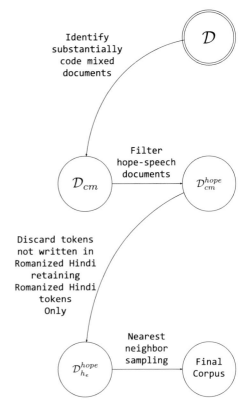

References

1. Alphabet, Inc. (2021) Hate speech policy. YouTube https://support.google.com/youtube/answer/2801939
2. Attenberg J, Melville P, Provost F (2010) A unified approach to active dual supervision for labeling features and examples. In: Balcázar JL, Bonchi F, Gionis A, Sebag M (eds) Machine learning and knowledge discovery in databases. Springer, Berlin, pp 40–55
3. Attenberg J, Ipeirotis P, Provost F (2011) Beat the machine: challenging workers to find the unknown unknowns
4. BBC News (2021) Kashmir attack: tracing the path that led to pulwama. BBC News https://www.bbc.com/news/world-asia-india-47302467
5. Buyse A (2014) Words of violence: "fear speech," or how violent conflict escalation relates to the freedom of expression. Hum Rights Q 36(4):779–797. http://www.jstor.org/stable/24518298
6. Chen Y, Mani S (2011) Active learning for unbalanced data in the challenge with multiple models and biasing. In: Guyon I, Cawley G, Dror G, Lemaire V, Statnikov A (eds) Active learning and experimental design workshop in conjunction with AISTATS 2010, JMLR Workshop and conference proceedings, Sardinia, Italy, Proceedings of machine learning research, vol 16, pp 113–126, http://proceedings.mlr.press/v16/chen11a.html
7. Conneau A, Lample G, Ranzato M, Denoyer L, Jégou H (2017) Word translation without parallel data. arXiv preprint arXiv:171004087
8. Conneau A, Khandelwal K, Goyal N, Chaudhary V, Wenzek G, Guzmán F, Grave E, Ott M, Zettlemoyer L, Stoyanov V (2019) Unsupervised cross-lingual representation learning at scale. arXiv preprint arXiv:191102116
9. Culliford E, Paul K (2020) Facebook offers up first-ever estimate of hate speech prevalence on its platform. Reuters https://www.reuters.com/article/uk-facebook-content-idINKBN27Z2QY
10. Culotta A, McCallum A (2005) Reducing labeling effort for structured prediction tasks. In: AAAI
11. Dagan I, Engelson SP (1995) Committee-based sampling for training probabilistic classifiers. In: Prieditis A, Russell S (eds) Machine learning proceedings 1995, Morgan Kaufmann, San Francisco, pp 150–157. https://doi.org/10.1016/B978-1-55860-377-6.50027-X. https://www.sciencedirect.com/science/article/pii/B978155860377650027X
12. Davidson T, Warmsley D, Macy M, Weber I (2017) Automated hate speech detection and the problem of offensive language. In: ICWSM
13. Ertekin S, Huang J, Bottou L, Lee Giles C (2007) Learning on the border: active learning in imbalanced data classification. In: CIKM 2007 - Proceedings of the 16th ACM conference on information and knowledge management, International conference on information and knowledge management, Proceedings, pp 127–136. https://doi.org/10.1145/1321440.1321461, 16th ACM conference on information and knowledge management, CIKM 2007; Conference date: 06-11-2007 Through 09-11-2007
14. Facebook, Inc. (2021) Facebook community standards: objectionable content hate speech. Facebook. https://www.facebook.com/communitystandards/objectionable_content
15. Jacobs J, Potter K (1997) Hate crimes: a critical perspective. Crime Justi Rev Rese CRIME JUSTICE 22. https://doi.org/10.1086/449259
16. KhudaBukhsh AR, Bennett PN, White RW (2015) Building effective query classifiers: a case study in self-harm intent detection. In: Proceedings of the 24th ACM international on conference on information and knowledge management. Association for Computing Machinery, New York, CIKM '15, pp 1735–1738. https://doi.org/10.1145/2806416.2806594. https://doi.org/10.1145/2806416.2806594
17. KhudaBukhsh AR, Palakodety S, Carbonell JG (2020) Harnessing code switching to transcend the linguistic barrier. In: Bessiere C (ed) Proceedings of the twenty-ninth international joint conference on artificial intelligence, IJCAI-20, International joint conferences on Artificial Intelligence Organization, pp 4366–4374, special track on AI for CompSust and Human well-being

18. KhudaBukhsh AR, Palakodety S, Mitchell TM (2020) Discovering bilingual lexicons in polyglot word embeddings. CoRR abs/2008.13347. https://arxiv.org/abs/2008.13347, 2008.13347
19. Kim S, Song Y, Kim K, Cha JW, Lee GG (2006) MMR-based active machine learning for bio named entity recognition. In: Proceedings of the human language technology conference of the NAACL, companion volume: Short Papers. Association for Computational Linguistics, New York City, pp 69–72. https://aclanthology.org/N06-2018
20. Klein AZ, Sarker A, Cai H, Weissenbacher D, Gonzalez-Hernandez G (2018) Social media mining for birth defects research: a rule-based, bootstrapping approach to collecting data for rare health-related events on twitter. J Biomed Inf 87:68–78
21. Lample G, Ott M, Conneau A, Denoyer L, Ranzato M (2018) Phrase-based & neural unsupervised machine translation. In: Proceedings of the 2018 conference on empirical methods in natural language processing. Association for Computational Linguistics, Brussels, pp 5039–5049. https://doi.org/10.18653/v1/D18-1549. https://aclanthology.org/D18-1549
22. Lewis DD, Catlett J (1994) Heterogeneous uncertainty sampling for supervised learning. In: Machine learning proceedings 1994, Elsevier, pp 148–156
23. Pagliardini M, Gupta P, Jaggi M (2018) Unsupervised learning of sentence embeddings using compositional n-gram features. In: NAACL 2018—Conference of the North American Chapter of the Association for Computational Linguistics
24. Palakodety S, KhudaBukhsh AR, Carbonell JG (2020a) Hope speech detection: a computational analysis of the voice of peace. In: Giacomo GD, Catalá A, Dilkina B, Milano M, Barro S, Bugarín A, Lang J (eds) ECAI 2020—24th European conference on artificial intelligence. Frontiers in artificial intelligence and applications. IOS Press, vol 325, pp 1881–1889. https://doi.org/10.3233/FAIA200305. https://doi.org/10.3233/FAIA200305
25. Palakodety S, KhudaBukhsh AR, Carbonell JG (2020b) Voice for the voiceless: active sampling to detect comments supporting the Rohingyas. In: Proceedings of the AAAI conference on artificial intelligence, vol 34(01), pp 454–462
26. Pereira-Kohatsu JC, Sánchez L, Liberatore F, Camacho-Collados M (2019) Detecting and monitoring hate speech in twitter. Sensors (Basel, Switzerland) 19
27. Saha P, Mathew B, Garimella K, Mukherjee A (2021) Short is the road that leads from fear to hate": Fear speech in Indian WhatsApp groups. In: Proceedings of the web conference 2021. Association for Computing Machinery, New York, WWW '21, pp 1110–1121
28. Scheffer T, Decomain C, Wrobel S (2001) Active hidden Markov models for information extraction. In: Hoffmann F, Hand DJ, Adams N, Fisher D, Guimaraes G (eds) Advances in intelligent data analysis. Springer, Berlin, pp 309–318
29. Settles B (2009) Active learning literature survey
30. Sindhwani V, Melville P, Lawrence RD (2009) Uncertainty sampling and transductive experimental design for active dual supervision. In: Proceedings of the 26th annual international conference on machine learning. Association for Computing Machinery, New York, ICML '09, p 953–960. https://doi.org/10.1145/1553374.1553496. https://doi.org/10.1145/1553374.1553496
31. Twitter, Inc (2021) Hateful conduct policy. Twitter https://help.twitter.com/en/rules-and-policies/hateful-conduct-policy
32. United Nations Office for the Coordination of Humanitarian Affairs (2021) Rohingya refugee crisis. YouTube. https://www.unocha.org/rohingya-refugee-crisis

Printed in the United States
by Baker & Taylor Publisher Services